Fishing the High Country

Also by WAYNE CURTIS

Fiction
One Indian Summer
Preferred Lies
Last Stand
River Stories
Monkeys in a Looking Glass
Night Train to Havana
In the Country
Homecoming

Non-Fiction
Currents in the Stream
Fishing the Miramichi
River Guides of the Miramichi
Fly-fishing the Miramichi
Wild Apples
Long Ago and Far Away
Of Earthly and River Things
Sleigh Tracks in New Snow

Poetry
Green Lightning

fishing the High Country

A Memoir of the River
WAYNE CURTIS

GOOSE LANE EDITIONS

Edited by Paula Sarson.
Cover and page design by Julie Scriver.
Cover image copyright © 2016 by Isabelle Levesque, isabellelevesque.com.
Printed in Canada by Imprimerie Gauvin.
10 9 8 7 6 5 4 3 2 1

Library and Archives Canada Cataloguing in Publication

Curtis, Wayne, 1943-, author
Fishing the high country : a memoir of the river / Wayne Curtis.

Issued in print and electronic formats.
ISBN 978-1-77310-083-8 (softcover).--ISBN 978-1-77310-084-5
(EPUB).--ISBN 978-1-77310-085-2 (Kindle)

1. Curtis, Wayne, 1943-. 2. Authors, Canadian (English)--20th century--Biography.
3. Fishers--New Brunswick--Miramichi River Valley--Biography.
4. Fly fishing--New Brunswick--Miramichi River.
5. Miramichi River Valley (N.B.)--Biography. 6. Autobiographies.
I. Title.

PS8555.U844Z42 2018   C813'.54   C2018-901271-4
                                               C2018-901272-2

We acknowledge the generous support of the Government of Canada,
the Canada Council for the Arts, and the Government of New Brunswick.

Goose Lane Editions
500 Beaverbrook Court, Suite 330
Fredericton, New Brunswick
CANADA E3B 5X4
www.gooselane.com

For Dennis Duffy

Fishing, brothers, is the greatest joy of my life. I don't ask for bread; only let me sit and hold a fishing-line.

"Dreams," Anton Chekhov

Introduction

MORE THAN A SPORT

I come from a long line of river people: boat pilots, log drivers, stuntmen, cabin builders, outfitters, canoeists, guides, and anglers. We have been living on the river Miramichi for two hundred years, seven generations. All of my forebears have been able of soul and body, and all have been blessed with the genes of longevity.

My great-great-grandfather John Curtis came from England in 1818. He swam the Miramichi at the Strawberry Marsh to meet his awaiting bride. Almost across, he realized he had forgotten the ring. So he went back, got the ring, and swam the river again.

David Curtis, his son, was a lumberman and riverboat pilot on the *Andover,* a sternwheeler that plied our river in the 1860s and '70s. Great-Grandfather knew every bar and boulder on the Miramichi that could be navigated—except, of course, in the upper reaches where the water was shallow. It was said of Great-Grandfather David that he was so strong he would put a barrel of flour under each arm and carry them up a steep hill from the boat to a store or farmhouse. During lumber booms, he carried deal from the big truck-wagons and loaded the tall ships moored at the wharves in Newcastle. David married Rebecca Harris, of Jewish descent, and they raised nine children.

I have only seen one photograph of the old man. It was taken in 1937, when he was a century old. His shoulders were sloped from many decades of carrying cargo; he had a long, flowing beard and resembled

Leonardo da Vinci's depiction of the Apostle Paul. It was said that at the age of 103, Great-Grandfather died while sitting on the front porch, reading a Bible without glasses and smoking his pipe. Having had his first taste of chewing tobacco at age three, he joked, he had abused the substance for over a hundred years. They said he would have lived to be an old man had he been able to kick his tobacco habit.

My grandfather Tom ("Papa"), David's son, was born in December of 1870. He was a log driver, a stuntman, and a scrapper. As an adolescent, he boxed, bare-fisted, with his brothers William, Charles, and Silas; he was supple of hand and foot, and, like his father, strong as an ox. With his hands in his pants pockets, he could kick nine feet high, leaving the hobnail prints of his driving boots on a beam in the thrashing barn. By the age of twenty-one, he had earned a fighting reputation. He fought at dance halls and even did battle to keep the respect of his sixteen-year-old wife, Barbara Sullivan, at the late-night charivari after they were married in Blackville's Holy Trinity Anglican Church in 1896. (This is the church where I was christened and in whose graveyard many of my kinfolk now rest.)

It was said that the whoops of the men on their wedding night awakened barnyards and brought working people to their windows. In the Miramichi of my grandfather's youth, rowdiness was in fashion.

After the wedding, Papa and Gram lived in Blackville—the Underwood property—for three years, until the spring of '99 when, with light hearts, they poled a white pine dugout canoe, loaded down with all their worldly possessions, five miles up the river to Keenan, where Tom had inherited a farm from his aunt, Sarah Nutbeam. Much of the farm was sheep pasture or meadowland that had never been touched by a plowshare or scythe. This is the farm where my father was conceived and born, in sight of the river. This is the beautiful country where I was born and raised, and where my river camp is located.

Introduction

It was said of Tom Curtis that he was a man's man: that he would never start a fight but would end one awfully quick. But I believe he actually liked combat, and throughout his long life, he had a boyish infatuation with that dangerous amusement. As a man in his seventies, he was still called upon to act as bouncer in dance halls, and in his mid-eighties, he would challenge this grandson in a boxing match. Papa was a show person, just as his oldest sister, Marguerite, had been. She moved to the United States in her early twenties and became an actress; she even performed at Carnegie Hall in October of 1910. Marguerite died in Boston on July 4, 1953, at the age of eighty-nine, and her remains were shipped back to the Miramichi by train. Yes, old Broadway lies in a churchyard here in Blackville.

As a young man growing up on the turbulent White Rapids stretch of the Miramichi River, my grandfather had learned how to turn handsprings on drifting logs, make a canoe out of a pine tree trunk, and throw a salmon spear into the reflections of a wire crew-pot in which a pitchwood fire illuminated the river's bottom to attract fish. He told me that he always speared his fish just in front of the back fin, which killed them instantly. Papa did this for the immediate family and the big cousinhood around White Rapids, supplying the fish for their winter's salt barrels.

With his first cousin Joe Smith, a trapper who later perished on Holmes Lake when he broke through a covering of November ice, Papa went to pools like the Salmon Hole on the Dungarvon River, a tributary of the Miramichi, via the Renous, or perhaps to Salmon Brook on the Cains. They would spear a truck-wagon load of fall salmon in one night, thus supplying a logging operation with a winter's salt fish. (There is a salmon mounted on a pine slab a yard wide and two yards long hanging over the mantelpiece in my cabin. It was caught in Papa's day, and mounted by Jim Dale, a taxidermist and undertaker who had a shop in Blackville. That salmon would have weighed over forty pounds.)

I can remember the old man telling me stories in vivid detail of those all-night adventures: the big, rugged men; the great wood-spoked truck-wagons; the able draft horses in blinders labouring under the harness as they hauled the night's catch along the old portage roads to the clink of shod hooves, deeper into the pine woods, further to the lumber camps, on some log-driving stream, perhaps the North Pole—a tributary of the Little Southwest Miramichi—or the North Branch of the Renous, where the cooks awaited his fish for the crew.

Papa's cousin Joe was a poet, a published songwriter, and a singer of folk ballads even then. Papa said that Joe Smith could make a groan deep in his throat that resembled a church organ. When they were travelling on those fish wagons through the woods, they would stop for a little nip. Then Joe played the organ and Papa would sing—songs such as "Peter Emberley" written by John Calhoun, Papa's upriver contemporary, and "A Winter on Renous" written by Smith himself. (These songs are now enshrined in the folklore of this province and are included in most anthologies of song and verse.)

My father, John Curtis, was born in 1911, the youngest son of Tom and Barbara. (They raised twelve children in all.) Daddy was also by nature a river man. But my father was never a fighter; rather, he was indifferent to such foolishness, the kindest, most passive man I ever knew. In his early years, he was a farmer/woodsman. He was also a singer of country ballads and a night drifter for salmon. Then he became an angler and later on an outfitter/guide. He turned into a conservationist. He loved all plants and animals and would not kill anything bigger than a mosquito.

During the Great Depression, my father and his neighbours netted their fall salmon. The Miramichi River and her tributaries were teeming with salmon in those days, and that is a good part of why my family settled here and, in fact, still lives here. Like the lumber trade and the farmlands, the river and the Atlantic salmon were a major source of our livelihood, our culture, and our spirit, just as the songs proclaim. Farming and fishing were the only means of survival during the 1930s. Sometimes they sold a few fish to the train men for money to buy tea, sugar, or tobacco, or maybe just enough pocket change to get into a dance. Mostly, though, they fished to fill the winter's salt cask.

Using a ten-fathom, fine-twine gillnet on clear fall nights, they drifted past our farm, down around that big bend in the river below the mouth of the Cains, that section of river the sport anglers now refer to as the Golden Horseshoe. My father and his neighbours filled their big board boats—which were difficult to pole against the currents—with salmon and grilse. They unloaded their catches on the flood meadows near our farmhouse, to be divided equally among the crew, and distributed them by means of a long-shafted, home-built wheelbarrow, a tin lantern on its front, blinking along from farm to farm. The slime-covered fish sloshed around in the concave wheelbarrow's box, the iron wheel crunched the sod, and the men's gumboots slipped and slid on the frosty grass as they clutched the shafts and struggled to keep the load from tipping over.

The men always caught their salmon after the oats had been harvested because the fall-run fish was not so fat and considered better for salting. During those cool nights of drifting, a woman was posted on a hillside, in a place where she could see up the river for a long way. If she saw lawmen approaching by canoe, if she saw wardens riding across the moon, she would fire a shotgun into the air so the men would have time to get their nets, their fish, and their boats off the water before the authorities arrived. But there were not many wardens in those days, and it was understood that the river people would get their winter's food supply in this way come fall. Later, we filled our salt barrels with salmon legally by fly casting.

When I was a child in the late forties and early fifties, I already had an infatuation with angling. In truth, I had been fishing long before I started school. At this time, the art of angling was for me in its most primitive stages. But during those primary years, I had an unconscious love of nature, and of course I hated the classroom. Beautiful as they were, I despised those early September mornings when I had to walk to Keenan School to be imprisoned for another long day. It was an age to be out of doors, a romantic time of year. The sun was yellow and cool winds blew across our reaped fields, the purple crabapples were dropping from the trees, and the bark of rifles could be heard in the woods behind the school. I can still hear the sound of those guns, see in their echoes the white-tailed deer on the run.

I can smell the dampness of morning dew on the schoolhouse steps, the stale bread and jam sandwiches, the chalk and musty book odours enshrouded in a veil of discipline around the desk of my aunt Lillian Underwood, a no-nonsense figure who had been teaching in that classroom since my father's schooldays. (She is telling me how to line my new scribbler with a ruler, and I can smell her body odour under the mask of perfume.) It was not easy to keep my mind on an assignment when the winds were making the big river sparkle and dance outside the schoolroom windows. Because according to the adults, this was the time of year when the push was on to fill the salt barrels with deer meat and salmon.

After we had sung "God Save the King" and "The Maple Leaf Forever," and while Aunt Lillian read the lessons, I daydreamed about being on the shore, at some eddy shaded by a pine tree. Or maybe casting from my father's old board boat, moored at the shore in front of home. (There were six feet of water at the outer end of that boat.) In those silent dreams, I could see down into that water where salmon and trout swam past me like shadows against washed gravel, and the chubs hung motionlessly in the currents to dart at my baited hook.

To get bait, I would have walked behind my father, picking up angleworms as he plowed the garden with a slew-footed old horse that had never worn shoes, and then I would run to the river, where the scent of blossom was strongest. Those fish were jumping, always jumping. The big silver fish in the air, oh so briefly, the two-fold splash. Like Daddy, I had a romantic imagination.

Even now those images keep me bound to a half-forgotten past, the days before I had a decent tackle, when everything river-related was bigger than real life. They were illusions I was trying to make real.

⌒

I hooked and landed my first salmon on June 4, 1951. The evening sky was an unmixed blue, white cloudlets adrift, the breeze blowing the snow-white blossoms from the bird cherry trees to sprinkle the river with confetti that floated past, as I stood waist-deep without wading boots and cast my fly hook into the boils of Papa's Rock. I was eight years old and in grade two. Having bought a split bamboo rod, a reel, and line from a mail-order catalogue a month before, I had learned how to cast the tapered line so the fly hook would hit the water and move like a real insect.

On this occasion, I had stolen away to the river, as country boys will when the farm chores are finally done and the outside world is so far away. I can still remember the big splash when that salmon came to the surface to take my fly, the pull from below, the upending leaps, the long downriver runs that made the line burn my fingers, the eventual exposure of the tip of its tail and dorsal fin as it tired. All of which meant that if things went according to plan and the tackle stood up, my family would be eating salmon boiled or fried at suppertime the next evening. It was a big salmon, but I don't know how much it weighed because it was not our custom to weigh a fish. The experience made that fish the size it was, and the size that is now remembered, enhanced no doubt, by the brushstroke of nostalgia. The excitement of catching my first salmon alone proved further seductive, and I spent all my free time either fly-fishing or thinking about the river. There was not much else to do in the country of my childhood.

Sometimes I shared my new tackle with a cousin who, when we caught a salmon, made sure that it was divided between the families. Sometimes these fish were shared with a classmate. In those days, my school chums and I used to argue about which was the best sport, salmon angling or partridge hunting, for we were all passionate lovers of rod and gun and were saving our pennies toward the purchase of both. But I can no longer grasp that old day, not with the same anxiety or carefreeness. Nor can I retrieve the feelings of triumph after a successful outing, either real or imagined. I suppose those special moments would have come out of a "time of life" more than anything, a day when all such encounters were the first of their kind, enhanced by the gift of originality. As happens through life, the youthful experiences, even the recollections of indifference, are eventually coloured by romanticism, so that no such amusements can truly be relived with the same nuance and passion. I guess Sergei Aksakov said it best: "Old bottles will not hold new wine, and old hearts are unfit to bear the feelings of youth."

By the late fifties my father had built a log cabin on the riverbank in front of our farmhouse and had become a small-time outfitter. We were depending more and more upon the fish as commerce, though my father's sport fishers were never money people, and some actually left camp in the night without paying for their lodging or my mother's fine meals. As a gofer around the sports, I picked up some of their ideas about angling, along with a tobacco addiction that haunts me to this day. I also got some hand-me-down equipment, including flies, hip waders, and a long-handled gaff, which was legal in those days, before hook-and-release became law. But in our family, fly-fishing for salmon had become more than just a sport: salmon remained a big part of our survival.

I can still see the big wooden barrels that stood in our summer kitchen, the bags of coarse salt, hard as rocks. I can see my grandfather in a butcher's apron, whetting his knife, a few salmon lying on the floor's wide boards to be split down the back so that their bellies and heads could be filled with salt and layered in a barrel. I still think of salmon in terms of barrels, not schools, not pounds, not inches—and certainly not held up in a photograph. For Papa told us never to take a picture of a dead or dying fish, that it was sacrilegious to do this to a species so sacred to our well-being. Besides, they all looked alike to us, filled with the same rock salt and layered in the same barrel. Bigger fish simply meant we would have to catch fewer of them. In that sense, salmon angling had become just another farm chore.

Sometimes, even now, when I am at a social gathering and am served smoked salmon, I think of my grandfather, the huge staved casks of salt fish and the old smokehouse with its crooked stovepipe. I close my eyes and try to recapture those special boyhood days. I think of when we went fishing in the early morning and that old summer kitchen, with its rough board walls, whitewashed, the hand-hewn beams, pots and pans hanging on nails above a giant wood-burning range with its simmering teapot, and the wood-handled clothes irons, still warm from the night before. The summer kitchen was covered with grey, weathered cedar shingles. It was semi-attached to the house, its windows framed with morning glory. Potted flowers stood on the windowsills, a custom from my mother's side of the family. I think of Papa in his flannel shirt, his sleeves rolled up; the wide, sweat-stained suspenders; the straw hat tilted over one ear; the drooping moustache; the straight-stemmed pipe. He might have been a character out of William Faulkner's Mississippi.

I recall with pleasure taking a drive to Blackville with Grandfather for more salt, five miles over a dirt road to Quinn's Mercantile, rattling along in the old half-ton, with a fox tail fixed to its hood ornament and windows that would not crank down. Twice, I had to grab the steering wheel to keep the truck on the road while Papa lit his pipe, coughing and puffing to fill the cab with smoke. The old man was singing "It Was I Who Killed the Cock Robin," a song from his youth. That day, Papa was as good-natured as I had ever seen him and, I suspect, as happy as he dared to be without bad luck following, for he was superstitious when it came to fun and laughter.

Of course, by that time, my grandfather was ninety years old. His voice had lost much of its power, and he was easily silenced into long periods of sleep, even as he sat upright in the truck (another reason to grab the wheel), or at home in his rocking chair, where he woke up from his fits of coughing, his eyes tearful. His Herculean strength had vanished with the ravages of time, and his thinning hair was white as cotton. I can remember every wrinkle in the old man's face. It had become a work of art itself.

"We need rain. Bring in new fish," he said without taking his eyes off the road, and I suspected to take my mind off his coughing frenzy.

"Bring in new fish," I nodded.

In the village, on the upriver clapboard wall of the store, there was a big tin sign — with a bucking bronco trademark — advertising the vintage Ogden's Fine Cut tobacco. The door opened with a jingle. Inside the shop, with its varnished wainscoting and pressed-tin ceiling,

I smelled the hampers of citrus fruit, the bulk candies, and the giant cans of tobacco that lined the shelves. Over by the soda fountain, there were jelly beans in a jar from which I bought ten cents' worth.

After Papa had gone out to the truck, the people who stood around the store — men who respected Papa, or perhaps had, at one time, feared him — asked, "How is your grandfather? How's the old man?"

"He's okay, I guess. He's okay, but... oh, he's... he's not too..." I shook my head and looked at the floor. Instantly I was ashamed that I had talked about Papa behind his back, possibly even to an old antagonist. And I could feel nothing but love and pity for my aged grandfather because, of course, he was *not* okay: he was nearing death. He slept a bigger portion of every day, and when he died on a stormy night that winter, my brothers and sister and I dug his grave, picking through a bed of frozen shale in the old Blackville cemetery, so he could rest in peace beside his sister Marguerite. I can remember thinking that nature has a beauty all its own, even in winter — especially in winter. It has a way of erasing all unpleasant impressions from an old day of hard work and worry. My grandmother, eight years his junior, followed him to the grave eleven years later.

The rains came and new fish came up the river, salmon whose ancestors would have been pursued by my forebears, who had failed to capture them. My older brother, Winston, was the fly-tier in the family. Using the old-fashioned bait hooks, off-set, with the straight eyes, he put together a combination of homemade patterns with my mother's black thread; fingernail polish; yarn; hen and duck feathers; squirrel tails; and bear, dog, goat, and calf hair. Some he constructed into slow-water designs with hackles that breathed and came to life, even skipped, when retrieved properly on the desired cast and swing. Win also tied the dry flies, the bombers and the streamers, from the tails of deer and moose. And even today when I see patterns that are nearly his in catalogues or in the showcases of the big sporting goods stores, I think that maybe my brother could have invented them.

Through trial and error, my brothers, sister, and I had learned how to fish the proper angles of casts: the speed of retrieve the fly hook required on the ninety-, seventy-five-, or forty-five-degree swing; the different strokes we practised in the pickup; the different pull and release in the false cast; the shoot—and sometimes a combination of all these skills—that a given stretch of water demanded if we were to hook and land our day's quota of salmon. There was the hit-and-move presentation, the beaver stroke, the floating drift, and the slow underwater swing, with some or no hand action. And there was the lazy forty-five-degree cast that is so commonly used today and is taught in fly-fishing schools as a fundamental for the novice angler.

But we had learned, perhaps through desperation, the more effective angles and speeds, and we knew the water and could divine where a salmon would be resting, if it was on the take, and what the fish demanded before it would strike and eventually be dragged by the gills up the hill. For we had learned to think like salmon. And each one of us brought our own personality to the quest, our own country distinctiveness of character. There was nothing uniform or academic here, save for the rod and reel.

My brothers, sister, and I fly-fished every evening after school, on Saturdays, and on holidays. (We were not allowed to fish on Sundays as my grandfather was a closet Baptist.) The Miramichi is a big river where it flows past our farm, so we had to learn how to cast long and straight in all conditions—wind, rain, or sleet—if the salt barrel was going to be filled. In the fall of the year, the push was on, and sometimes when the end of the season was drawing near and the cask still half empty, my brothers and I jigged school. I can remember one morning after the school bus had gone, Winston and I stole away to the river, where we caught eight salmon before noon. When, at dinnertime, we carried these fish up the hill and into the summer kitchen and laid them on the floor, my grandfather was happy and set out to fillet them for the barrel. But my mother was furious because we had not got on the bus. She told us that she did not want to see her children grow up in ignorance, and that because we were poor, we'd have to work harder to break new ground. My mother had grown up in the country, but she was a good reader and did not preach the old country ways. While she had a vocation for the learned life, she never had the opportunity to pursue it. In her own words, "Where I went to school, the teachers didn't seem to know much themselves, and even had a prejudice toward educated people."

Some years, if the barrel was not filled by the time the angling season ended, we kept right on fishing. The biggest fish I ever caught was a twenty-two-pound hen salmon. With my brother Gary watching for the fish wardens, this big salmon was hooked at dusk in the old home pool on October 2, 1958. On that worn-out tackle, it had been an hour-long struggle to bring it to shore. When I took my catch to the next farm to show it to my uncle Eldon, he said, "Cripes! I thought the fishing season had closed last week." He was coming out of the woods after an evening of deer hunting.

⸻

I started my career as a river guide in the summer of '59. Hughie Phaff, a man from Vermont, was staying at my father's camp. After just one day, he had become a close friend to the family and was getting a reduced rate. In the evening, he stood with my father beside Mother's piano, drank his Scotch whisky, and sang the old country songs of Hank Williams, like "Your Cheating Heart" and "Lost Highway." The next morning, he asked me if I knew the river and where could we go to find him a salmon.

"I don't know," I told him. "Let's have a go at Papa's Rock, and we'll see what happens."

He waded out to his waist and started casting into the boils the big rock made near centre stream. I saw a splash and heard him shout, "Hey, lad, I got one on!"

He hooked three grilse that morning before ten and was a happy camper. Of course, when it came to that stretch of water, I knew the music it would make if fished properly from top to bottom, and was not just repeating the instructions I'd read by note; I learned through trial and error, a whole childhood on the river. I guided the man for three falls, even though I was underage and had no guide's license. Each year, along with my wages of five dollars a day, he tipped me with a carton of Camel cigarettes. When he returned for the fourth fall, I had already moved on to the city to look for winter's work in a shoe store.

Still, over the next fifty years, I guided a good part of every angling season. I have worked for all of the major outfitters along the Miramichi, and some not so major. You learn a lot about a river that way—standing in the water, instructing the fishers to do what comes naturally to those of us who grew up here. It is funny how brain surgeons or rocket scientists can hang themselves if you put a fishing rod in their hands.

One fall, a woman from the Doctors Island Fishing Lodge taught me how to barbecue a salmon over hardwood coals, roasting it flesh-side down for twenty minutes, with only salt and pepper added. We did this every day for two weeks, leaving the island lodge without a lunch, depending upon my guiding advice and her casting arm to provide us with the midday meal. That doctor was a genuine character and had a flare for originality. She would try anything. As hunger overtook us, we discussed strategies in a series of metaphors that were intelligible only to ourselves, until we had a fish, by hook or by crook, dragged upon the gravel shore. This was back in the day when Marilyn Monroe was said to have been fishing here. During those autumn cookouts, I kept an eye on passing canoes in hopes of getting a glimpse of her. I never saw her, nor did anyone I talked to along the river. But even today, when I have a family barbecue at Camp Oriole, I cook my salmon in that way. It has become my signature dish. The scent of salmon roasting and the melancholy of an old country song still conjure images, first of my father with his Serenade guitar, and then of Marilyn Monroe—not on the river for sure, but in the movies.

Not all of my guests were that much fun to be around. At Wade's Fishing Lodge, an undertaker from New York who was a heavy boozer threatened to bury me that evening if we did not have a fish in the boat by five o'clock. Our party of six anglers and their guides were lunching at midday on the shore at the Oxbow Pool on the Cains.

When the senior guide, John Brophy, overheard these words, he said to the New Yorker, for all to hear, "We bury undertakers in this river too! Now did you come here to fish or to fight?"

"No, no, to fish!" he snapped with astonishment. "I came to fish." The old undertaker calmed down after that, and I had no more trouble with him. But understanding how passionate he was about catching a salmon, I was feeling a kind of pressure I had not previously experienced, not even in the hungry days of fishing for the supper table. For when you are a guide, you want to do your job well, develop a reputation that will attract future clients. So at four thirty, I asked him if I could try his rod. We did get a fish that afternoon and my life was spared. Still, the undertaker left disgruntled, and without leaving a tip. It was great to see the back of him.

At Black Rapids Lodge, while trying to scoop an angler's salmon—his first one in a week of casting—I fell into the river right over my head, and when my waders filled with water, I had to be helped to shore, coughing.

"No need to drown yourself," my guest told me, laughing. "It's only a fish. I am here mostly for the conversation anyway."

At the Miramichi Inn on the Little Southwest, I had a wading angler drift away in the heavy currents of the Foran Rapids. He had not heard what I told him above the roar of the water and had gone out too far. He would have drowned had I not been able to run down the shore, wade out and grasp his arm, and drag him onto the gravel beach. He was as lifeless as a rag and overtired from battling the intake of water.

Along with him, I have saved at least one other man from drowning over the years. And there was one I could not save. On April 26, 1971, Dr. Niles Perkins of Bowdoinham, Maine, went into the water when his boat overturned in the big river, which was just two degrees above freezing. With heavy clothes on, you can't swim in water like that, and he went under before any of us guides could get to him.

There are no bravery medals or accolades for river guides — not like the police, not like the search-and-rescue units, not like the military. For the guide, it's all in a day's work, calamity, storms, and high water notwithstanding. There is no union protection against abusive clients or outfitters who seek guarantees, no curfews on working hours, no liability rules when it comes to river or weather hazards, no counselling after a fatal tragedy. It is all left to the guides to talk it out among ourselves — in the way that my uncles got together to talk out the bad parts of the war before they could put it to rest. Or to even write about it before it leaves our conscious minds and is forgotten. And there is that old river wisdom: when you are on the water with a guest, everything that can go wrong will go wrong.

However, most of my professional river experiences were memorable and without calamity. Through the years — especially in those days when I was writing for Tourism New Brunswick — I guided or fished with such fishing celebrities as Jim and Sylvia Bashline, Stan Bogdan, Gary Borger, Art Flick, Gene Hill, Jim Lorentz, Gary Loomis, Joan and Lee Wulff, and Ted Williams. All were pleasurable to be with, and our river days together were far too few.

⟨⟩

My own river camp, built in 1974, sits on a section of the old home property I had inherited from my father and mother. Daddy and I used white pine logs, the corners notched into dovetails. It is a good, solid cabin with a stone fireplace. In back of the camp yard is a swampy meadow, with bog holes and hillocks and tall poplar trees, where the leaves dance from the river winds, and from where the musical phrases of birds, toads, and frogs colour the air. Out front, on breezy days, the broad, slow-moving river shimmers like a sheet of steel under the sun's reflections. In the evenings, perhaps after a shower that has turned our weather-beaten farm buildings from grey to black—the most beautiful time of day—the shoreline trees reflect on the mirror-smooth water. And I can see, from my seat on the veranda, the salmon that school past.

Through the years, when I was not working as a guide, I fished with my sons, Jeff, Jason, and Steven. They were just small boys in the seventies, but on the river, I could see in them a part of my early self, my father, and my grandfather. In mid-June, when the schools were closed for the summer, we would leave our modern home in the estuary and move to the cabin, where we stayed until September. This was our little provincial universe with its own centre of gravity, and we did not want to leave it. We fished those old home waters for weeks running, and sometimes we took three-day excursions to tributaries such as the North Pole Stream, the Dungarvon, or the Cains, tenting along the shores of those wonderful salmon rivers, cooking hot dogs and brewing tea on open campfires.

Other times we left the cabin and hiked to Morse Brook, where we fished Aunt Edith's Hole, or to the big beaver dams up in back of our old property lines. (My great-aunt Edith had been a lover of trout angling and went there often on summer vacations during the fifties when she was home from Duluth, Minnesota.) We got trout for the breakfast frying pan. The logging roads in back of the camp, where as a boy I had lumbered and hunted deer with my father, though overgrown, were still easy to follow, and sometimes we chanted the lyrics of an old country song on our way, following the converging wheel ruts. Having the boys along on these little expeditions, having them experience the same things that I did as a youngster, meant all the world to me.

My then-wife, the late Janet Manderville, must have been a saint to tolerate so much frivolous river talk — the comparing of tackle, the technique used on such-and-such a water, and the river's geography and character in general. For these river subjects monopolized the conversations around the dinner table. Sometimes she came with us on canoe runs down the Cains or Renous, when we paddled through the long days and made camp on the shore, where we fought flies with the smoke of a campfire stinging our eyes. Some days we battled an upriver wind for hours on end before we got to our destination. So as time went on, Janet's trips with the family became more and more seldom, as she appeared to be indifferent to the raggedness of the terrain and the elements. But on those outings, all three of my sons hooked and landed their first salmon by the age of eight. And of course they had cranked in many sea-run brook trout. It was just a re-enactment of the old tradition. And our love for the river, and each other, was like an addiction we had no desire to overcome.

Those were wonderful days, when my boys were small and my mother and father were still well and active and came to our cabin for birthday parties and fondues. We had big celebrations on the year's closing day. We compared our river diaries to see who had out-fished whom. Sometimes at those parties, I showed a film of Lee

Wulff fly-fishing—with light tackle— on Newfoundland's Portland Creek in the 1940s. (In later years, Lee became a friend and was my sponsor when I joined the Outdoor Writers Association of America.) Or maybe I showed a film that featured Ted Williams, formally of the Boston Red Sox, who lived near our cabin in those days and whom I had fished with many times. Sometimes it was a kitchen party with fiddling, step-dancing, and singing. Even today the songs of John Denver and Joni Mitchell carry in their melodies images from that special time.

Back then, during my own summer holidays, I would sit on the veranda by a card table and write articles for those wildlife magazines you see in tobacco shops. (On their covers, the mule deer have exaggerated antlers, and the fish are so much bigger and wilder than anything in real life.) It was before the age of computers, and I was using an old iron Remington typewriter with letters that would not punch out clearly and a cylinder that jammed the paper. I had to hammer down the keys with one finger. I still type that way.

In the heat of the afternoon, I sometimes took a break from my work and went to the river where the children were swimming. And I would sit in the coolness of the tall shore grass, soon to fall under my father's scythe, and observe the scene as a kind of research. This was where, in Papa's day, the big log jams crowded the river from shore to shore, and the young men ran on them in shows of bravado: to drop through meant certain death. This was where our team of horses broke through the ice while pulling the bobsleds loaded with two cords of maple stovewood, my grandfather shouting, "We gotta throw the wood off, before we lose sleds and all!" The horses and crew survived the incident unharmed, but it was touch and go for a while. This was where, at twilight one August evening, I watched a black bear grab a salmon from the shallows and run with it into the trees. The fish had gone into the mouth of McKenzie Brook, where the water was colder, but very shallow. And I can still see the long-abandoned farmhouse on the opposite hillside, now screened by a stand of poplar trees, where I attended my first wake, the coffin still in the parlour. I can hear my father's words, "That's the first time I ever saw Jim Campbell all dressed up."

Even now, especially now, the natural images offer a kind of prose that is beyond words. We, the river people, are so much a part of the landscape, the riverscape that we inhabit and that controls our moods and dreams. The river lands have the power to hold us on course. It might be through something as subtle as a crow's fleeting shadow as it glides across a country lane; the melancholy of a mission bell, remote on the breeze; or the setting sun that shines through a broken cloud to make golden wheel spokes in the sky. Indeed, there is no language to describe the heart-shared feelings conveyed by such images to those who are oblivious to the sounds and senses, so can never perceive them. This is a language only for the ones who have witnessed the experiences, shared the passion and the river spirit.

By this time, things have changed from the days of fly-fishing for the salt barrel. Times are better, so there is no desperation, no pressure to bring home a fish for the supper table. Angling for Atlantic salmon has become instead a chance to practise something entrenched in our bloodstreams for generations. Hook-and-release laws have come into effect, so we no longer drag a fish of any size up the hill. The equipment has also changed to the ultra-modern, lightweight rods that will throw a fly hook farther than I ever dreamed of doing as a young man. Lines, leaders, and reels are modernized. And of course it is a different river today, too, with fewer fish that come in mostly on the rise after rainstorms because the water drops off quickly to the height, warmth, and smell of the old dog days, even in high summer.

This can make life difficult for my son Jason, now a professional river guide, as he tries to please a client who has booked his fishing trip months in advance. The quality of the angling is hard to predict, even for long-standing river people. But this is still a beautiful river, its waters clear and as cold as iced ammonia, with an excellent sea-run trout population and a superb salmon fishery that help drive the river's economy.

On special occasions, like Father's Day or perhaps a family birthday, we celebrate at the river camp. My grandsons, Samuel and Joshua, come with their father and uncles. The boys are in their first years of high school, but already they are experienced river people and are outfitted with modern equipment, including life jackets, sunscreens, and other protective devices that, as a boy, I never would have thought of owning. In the summer of 2013, my grandson Samuel, the oldest, hooked and landed his first Atlantic salmon.

When we are fishing together, I look at them, each making the long cast, experimenting with the angles, practising the retrieve, the drift, sometimes even a mend — though I never believed in mending, not for this fish. Rather, I preach the straight cast, with a swing like the pendulum of a grandfather's clock. Watching them, I can see a part of myself.

In the past few years, I have turned down many would-be clients. While I need the money and indeed the camaraderie of new acquaintances, I find the mental and physical strain is too taxing on my time-worn body and soul. Having suffered one near heart attack, I no longer have the stamina to work as a river guide, to travel the long days, in and out of the water, up and down the steep inclines to and from the cabins, poling loaded canoes against the currents. I can now only dream of getting to the places where I used to angle with success. But the aches and pains in my bones keep the presence of those waters flowing around me, even as I write this.

Nowadays, I stay in camp and observe through its big window fronting the river the scenery and any activity that may be happening on the old home river. I watch the out-of-country anglers standing in waist-deep water, casting, casting, their faces glowing against the sun's brilliance. I feel the mystery of their expectations, their anticipation of the moment that has brought them here—the splash, the big pull, the salmon's long run that will give them a youthful thrill.

In my night dreams, or the insomnia between dreams, I hear the anglers' barks, crisp and clear above the din of water. I see the bending rods, the yellow casting lines that cut the clear water like twine through vodka. And I jump to my feet in a panic, looking to give a hand in landing the fish, only to find that I am in my cabin, alone.

My Miramichi

Ask me why I live in Miramichi and I will tell you that I do because I was born here: this is my home. For sure, it is not easy to explain in a few short sentences the love one might have for the river and the land.

It is never simple to communicate—to non-river people, especially—the excitement that comes in the last days of winter, when those long-awaited south winds drift down the valley to make the pine trees whisper and start the ice melting, so that you have a strip of blue water, like matting on an unpainted canvas, along each shore. And you stand to watch the crows and the ravens, first yellow against the evening sun, then black as they flock down on the shaded ice to complete the canvas. It is difficult to describe the hope that comes with the narrow patches of brown grass exposed on riverbanks and knolls that look like moustaches on faces crusted in old shaving cream. There is no need to explain away the joy that comes with the sight of the first robin as it hops about on the pine straw or the earth-scented and soggy plowed land, or the familiar voices of Canada geese that may be heard but not seen as they fly high in the wavering *v*'s, downriver, toward the bay.

These little signs of renewal can trigger an awakening in the souls of river people who have been, to some extent, in hibernation since the aspens in the swamps turned from pea green to orange and the first snow of autumn fell upon us. These images blend together like a conspiracy of assuredness, signals informing us that the longest and coldest winter in fifty years is finally over and that spring is really here, though perhaps two weeks behind the calendar's date. (Another winter like that will lay us all in our graves, we think.)

It is almost impossible to communicate the soft warmth of a cabin on chilly April nights when you let the maple logs in your fireplace burn high to send blinking reflections against the log walls and picture frames, and the sweet aroma, along with the sounds of the crackling fire, are suddenly muted by the rumble of an ice floe that churns and crashes past the front door as it labours toward the distant sea. And how you rise, turtle-like, out of your Mark Trail sleeping bag and, tripping over furniture, hurry to the door to try to glimpse the moving jam, which is always so much louder, so much more dramatic in the darkness.

"Well, God be praised! Spring finally!" You talk to yourself in times like that. You hold the beam of your five-cell flashlight on the passing ice so you can be a witness and tell people tomorrow, "I saw her go boys, by home there, at three o'clock s'mornin'." And you wonder why the ice always goes out in the middle of the night when people are asleep in their eighth- or ninth-generation ancestral country houses. They are in sight of the river, yes, but too far away to feel the rumble.

It is out there on that big, dark river that the season is finally changing, and for river people, ice-out signals the official coming of spring. You go back to bed but you rest uneasy upon the covers while cursing the darkness, the slowness of the clock, because you are not exactly sure just how much damage the ice floes are doing to your bank trees. There are a thousand sounds in the river on a night like this; they elicit spooky images that make your imagination run wild. For reassurance, you envision yourself wading into the old home pool, making the long high cast, raising your first salmon on the fourth day of June 1951. You listen to the ice floes and relive that evening when you were eight years old. Yes, it is the same old river.

And I suppose I should tell you about the sense of wonder you feel when the moon lights up the drifting ice and holds it in a dazzling abstractness—like the old negatives we used to get with developed photographs, held to a light. This is eventually followed by a sunrise that makes the moving ice pink against a slow-moving glacier. In your mind, you fast forward the seasons to when the north wind turns the river into a meandering trickle of ink, the shore grass into straw, the bank trees into a hundred shades of reds and orange. And there is the spring brood of wild geese, like so many decoys bobbing on the water.

After a time of restless and uncertain wonder, you wake up in the early morning, feeling the strong sunshine beaming through your latticed windows to warm the bedclothes. And remembering the night's events (or was it a dream?), you rush to the front door to see that open water, ebbing and flowing and being tossed about by the upriver winds. As if they came from out of the water itself, there are ducks bobbing on the surface already. The river is a tapestry of blues and whites just now, appearing as unstable as a newborn calf. (It is moving more slowly than normal because there is an ice jam somewhere downriver.) In minus six degrees of frost, there is new slush drifting down, all the more beautiful this time around. But still, you know this is the day that you will listen for the whine and putter of motorboats, hear the whoops and the barks of the anglers and guides, the splash of jumping salmon, see the bowed rods and the taut fishing lines—with the descending beads of water dripping from them—glinting in the sunshine. And you think that of all the months of the calendar year, all the seasons of life, April is the most exciting time to be alive.

⌒

When we were children, in winter on that old river ice, we skated in games of hockey, practising our slapshots with an alder branch and the heel of a discarded shoe, dreaming of getting a call from the

Montréal Canadiens. After ice-out, when the water was still too high and treacherous for a youngster to go near it, we stood in the lee of the wind—on the upriver side of the mill shed, where the velvety old boards were warmed by the sun—and we watched the sport fishers all day long. Those kite winds of April wrinkled the water and made it a dark blue, while the big leafless elm trees creaked and groaned to spook us. But it was good to see the colours come back into the land and water, having spent so many months in an ashen world of snow. In the days before ice-out, we had walked the sun-warmed railroad line to the village—so remote in comparison—where we attended the western picture shows and the St. Patrick's concerts in the clapboard church hall, where there was fiddling and dancing.

Those old country stories and tunes, now outgrown, had stayed in our minds while we casted in the manure-stained field ponds with our make-believe fishing rods. We were filled with glee as we anxiously awaited the day when our mail-order tackle would arrive at the post office from Eaton's of Canada. In reality those items were always a disappointment compared to the catalogue photos. But now, of course, trying to resurrect these moments of early childhood is like attempting to recall a life before an incarnation.

While you make tea and prepare to fix breakfast in the cabin's add-on kitchen on this new day in this new season, you keep an eye out the window toward that old blue river because she is such a novelty just now. You take the frying pan down from where it hangs on a nail behind the stove, lay some bacon strips across it, and too soon you smell the fat when it starts to sputter and curl into a burnt and smoky crispness—because you have forgotten to move the pan from the cover over the firebox, the hottest part of the stove—and the tea kettle is whistling as the open water distracts you from cooking. You shiver in the still-cool cook room and pour the tea and stare at the moving water, purple now, with its shoreline ice heaps that look like an ornate picture frame. And like old times, with a make-believe crayon, you unconsciously fill in the calendar scenes: the men and women huddled in green canoes, bending rods, scoop nets in the water, the salmon jumping over at the mouth of McKenzie Brook.

After breakfast you sit and drink tea and smoke tobacco and look out at the open river. The water, blue again, has brought with it a sense of wonder. The morning is agreeable and pleasant, and you circle the date on a calendar: "spring." You think of yourself as a kind of artist, because you see, hear, and feel things that others in the community may not notice. You have become accustomed to measuring these things in little pockets, moments that stay with you for years. And you feel in your bones this is one of them to be remembered. Like when you got the chance to dance briefly with your first love down at the Legion hall five years ago, and again on a Saturday night last spring. These things remain in a special corner of your memory, to be retrieved and relived once in a while.

But you are constipated when it comes to revealing these heart feelings to anyone.

On the night before, two of your brothers and a cousin had dropped in and brought their guitars. Together you talked of the late spring, the impending summer and fall, and you sang some old favourites, "Fisherman's Son," "Sonny's Dream," "Saltwater Joys." Now you can still hear the laughter and the music that is such a big part of your universe, it keeps you and your cousinhood connected. Play on, boys.

These sounds and the scents of Scotch whisky, marijuana smoke, and overflowing ashtrays are strong in the cabin, the inside stove still warm, as you set out to find some number one and number two bucktail streamers and a good, strong tapered leader. You take the old black salmon rod—your father gave it to you for Christmas in '65—down from the beams, and you attach the J.W. Young Pridex reel you inherited from your grandfather. It has long since qualified as an antique, but it still works well. (You cannot wear out those reels, not in one lifetime.) The old five-ounce fibreglass rod and the heavy reel are out of fashion, but you take them for tradition's sake—because of how you came by them, and because they have cranked in many salmon, both black and bright, and they have an element of good luck sealed beneath the scratched-up metal and sun-chipped varnish.

You grab your mackinaw coat from where it is hanging on a chair, go out into the soggy camp yard, and listen to the spring birds' chirping non-stop. Observing that it will be a clear day, you get into your mud-stained pickup truck with the farm licence plates, and you drive six miles over the snow-banked and bumpy gravel road, smoking and driving faster than you can ever remember doing—like smoking and driving fast go together—the truck whining when you shift down into second gear, with the front wheels pulling the truck into the long ruts filled with muddy water that splashes the windshield, the wiper blades leaving the semi-circle scrapes and scratches, the ditches having overflowed since late March. And there is the sour smell of tomcat urine and melting snow, discarded beer bottles and cans, the empty cigarette and fish-and-chip boxes exposed in the snowbanks.

You turn on the radio, which has its dial set on the local radio station CKMR. You listen to the news of the big ice jam downriver, where some homes and camps have been flooded. This is replaced by the harmony of Doc and Chickie Williams. You listen to the singing and picture them, not on the big stage at the Grand Ole Opry in Nashville, but rather at the local church hall when they were here on tour last fall.

You slow up as the truck bumps over the bare railway tracks and you look down the grade for the jitney that will bring the mail and the newspaper. You pass some little houses where dogs bark and chase after the truck. You wave at the skimpily clad children who wade in road ponds in their mismatched, wrong-footed rubber boots, because to not wave at the children is a show of arrogance to the family. The morning sun lights up their freckled faces and it shines under the high doorsteps of porches where the littered ground is bare. And there are the empty and broken-backed old barns—the untracked crust, purple around them—standing hard to the wind that always arrives with the open water. Past the schoolhouse hill there are the sagging pole-fenced lanes, ungraded under the morning sheen. On the upriver side of one barn, grey against brown, stands a rustic, two-horse farm wagon. Framed by the melting snow, it appears like a piece of folk art, or perhaps a giant monster that has crawled onto the bare grass and into the sunlight, having survived a prehistoric ice age. And there is a rusted spring-tooth harrow propped up against the wall. Smothered in the leafless clematis, it looks like a giant spider in its web.

The too-far farmhouse with its spooled verandas and grey sheds have long since vanished. You remember that old place with affection, having grown up in its shadows. You can still feel the warm spirit of the family, their generosity, their honesty. It is steeped into your soul. This was where, in your mid-teens, you caught a June salmon on a Bumble Bee fly hook when fishing trout at the falls below the stone railway bridge. And you shared it with the family.

You pass the three-mile pine tree—twice splintered by lightning—with its patch of orange-needled ground under it, and on past the snowed-over burnt woods with its piercing black stubs, the empty lumberyard and the closed-down sawmill with its idle gangway and crippled saw carriages, the long-armed gates blocking the already vandalized conveyers and pipes. And a little thought—a moment inspired perhaps by an odd-shaped tree, a fence post, or maybe a cloud formation—takes you two miles down the road as you unconsciously envision a time from long ago when you walked this snow-filled trail, in fine shoes and bare head, to get to a dance. Living in the moment that carries a thrust of ingenuity, you talk to yourself and laugh, right out loud, until a pond of brown water forces you to slow the truck again to a crawl, and your reflections drift back to reality: the warm spring morning, the river open now again.

"Thank the Lord it's here now, finally," you say out loud. "Yes, yes, yes, she's here at last. Now let's hope she holds and we get some cool nights so the water clears up." You turn off the radio to save the battery. Easing the truck onto the solid pavement with its broken frost-heaves, you turn off the key — to save fuel — and coast down the hill into the village, past Quinn's Mercantile, Bean's Variety, the old movie house (with its busted marquee), and the pool hall. The little white church spire towers above the bare-limbed trees, its Sunday knell spreading its spirit as you pull into the convenience store, get gas for the motor, and buy a fishing licence and a can of tobacco.

On the counter in the gas bar, there are doughnuts in a jar and an ashtray is overflowing with lipstick-stained cigarette butts. People elbow each other around the coffee makers.

You overhear someone say, "Boys, she's all jammed bank-high in the Rapids."

"We'll have high water yet! A lotta snow in the woods."

"Hard fishin' till she clears up."

"Ain't nobody not gonna get no fish a-tall 'fore next Sunday, I figger."

"You wouldn't get a fish if the river was full of them."

"I get me share when the ice is gone and they're runnin'."

"Well the ice is gone now, t'iz up home."

"He'd be a good tastin' lad fried up right about now too, wouldn't he."

"The very best."

"Yes, with a little molasses and homemade bread."

"A hard-times old fish, but this time a year, he'd taste pretty damned good . . ."

"I eat a lot worst."

"And you'll eat worst agin, too."

A Mountie—wooden-faced, slim, with the high boots, broad hat, and a gun in its holster—pulls up to the gas pumps and fills his tank before coming inside to pay for his purchase. While he is here, the men fall silent.

After he is gone, one of them says, "Wouldn't take a lad, would he? No he wouldn't. No he wouldn't."

You take your coffee outside, stand, roll and smoke cigarettes in the shimmer of the sunlight. You bump shoulders for approval of new ideas the spring has brought. Someone is heading to Alberta to do shift work in the oil fields and will be back in a month to guide. Another is going to work downriver on construction, coming home nights. Others are waiting for the sports to come to get some guiding.

"Boys, I wonder if she'll go down much by tomorrow mornin'. I got an old lad from Maine who wants to come the very day the ice leaves."

"If the bridge stays in, he might get here."

"How's he travelling? Bus? Big tipper is he?"

"No, no, he's no cheapskate."

"Boys, all that ice will go today. Papa said he saw it jam in the Rapids a hundred times and that's how she works."

"Then she'll start fallin'."

"Boys, a motorboat went up by home early s'mornin', right close to our side."

"He musta came down on the ice."

"Ha, ha, ha, ha, haaaa!"

"He wanted to get a first crack at them fish."

When I was an adolescent, on days like this, my school chums and I stole away from the schoolroom and fished with the "green permit" the wardens gave us free, immediately after ice-out. In truth, back then we started fishing—though illegally—in late March, when the first signs of open water appeared along the shores where spring-fed brooks flowed into the main river, and the winds were sweeping up the crusted valley at sunset to make pink caverns and turn the power lines along the road into fuzzy red cat's cradles. We stayed out of doors into the twilight of those lengthening spring days, while our mothers and fathers wallpapered and whitewashed our bedrooms—with the windows open—to make them look like the photos we had seen on paint cans or, indeed, the furniture catalogues where everything looked bigger and better than in real life. And later we knelt by our beds and said our prayers, glancing out the blindless windows at the sky, while praying for the whole family, listing off the names, Mummy, Daddy, Papa—remembering him in his coffin, hearing the funeral growl of the church organ—and Gram, for God to hear. That time also comes from a special place in the mind.

Now, having returned from the village, you slide the recently painted board boat over the bank and into the water, and watch as its leaks tighten up with the swelling. You set down the motor and the slopping, unbalanced gas can, and rig the anchor rope to the pulleys. Then you bundle up—because it is always much colder out there on the water—and head out across the now sparkling blue river with the water lapping under the chin of the boat and the sun warming the back of your winter jacket. Smoke sputters from the motor to unravel behind the boat like a vapour trail. It mixes with the cigarette smoke, the strong scent of gasoline.

You are throwing a line with the number two Mickey Finn over the side as you go. In the bend across from the camp, you cut the motor and ease out the anchor while the fishing line is still swinging long and deep, and you crank in slowly to the *tap, tap, tap* of the reel. The boat has swung on the anchor and is hanging steady against the currents when you feel the big pull, strong and deep! You lay back hard on your cork grip, hearing your grandfather's reel give a screech as the old California Fenwick bends double. You know that you are into a big spring salmon and that these fish are lean and mean—pound for pound as strong and as good a fighter as any fish in the world because they have the April waters and you have the April mindset with you.

I can't begin to tell you what kind of feeling it is to have that first salmon of the season on the end of your line, holding deep and circling the boat, with the heavy water working in its favour, while you—red-cheeked from the biting breeze and sun—crank and sway the rod, trying to bring the kipper-jawed, heavy-shouldered specimen to the surface, as you relive a thousand other fish battles, a million friendly toasts to the big one that did *not* get away, which this salmon's presence and its feel on the tackle brings. This, with the memory of the laughter and the music from last evening still playing in your mind, makes you feel like you are twenty years younger and could fish all day. For the moment, you live in the seasons that lie behind—the day before yesterday—and yes, ahead—the day after tomorrow.

Because you have been waiting so long for spring, these symbols, these traditions, fall upon you well behind the almanac's stubborn schedule. You have been living in this moment, the preliminary warm spell, since late March, early April. But you know that the bottomlands and elm-treed meadows will flood before real spring arrives.

⌣⟩

In our fields and woods, the sun and the oven winds are dissolving the mountains of snow. It melts from the top side to make an overnight crust that shines like porcelain under the red and yellow sunrises. And it decays from below to make tunnels and caverns like ant trails in a rotting sill. These and the gullies fill with urine-coloured water (from the barns) and overflow to push along in the ditches among rocks, rails, black ice, and grassy knolls, chuckling and steaming in a mist, baring the higher grounds and the oat-stubble flats. The willow trees drink up the moisture and give birth to rabbit paws of new hope—furry buds, white along black stems—that toss about like beads of jellybean, bitter in their taste but sweet in the scent of spring. The river rises equal to its banks, exceeding the flood meadows and the harrowed intervals, and the upriver ice drifts away, down by our place, in white rectangles and triangles of pale, washed-out marble. Some are like barn doors and some are pie-shaped kitchen tables under white cloths and some are faded blue skating rinks, stained with bonfire ashes. As if for assuredness, across the river a robin sings in the Elm Tree Meadow.

But then—as happens with spring in the northeast—snow comes again, this time mixed with smoking clouds of rain. It whitens and then blackens the old barns and makes the elm trees shiver. Suds of shampoo scour the fields of dirty blonde hair. Then it freezes to make little embroidered cliffs and caves that stand like granite upon the sheaves of dead grass that glisten pink in the cool morning sunlight. Until the downriver winds, scented with burning grass, come whispering through the screens of our bedroom windows. It lifts the hems of the curtains and scatters the crayoned sketches and the western comic books that lay on bedside tables. The black alder swamps at the edge of fields turn to purple and then to green, picking up spirits with the mouse's ear of new leaf. The spring salmon are jumping as they hurry back to the sea. And this time the metaphoric spring becomes a reality.

My Miramichi

I would not try to describe the excitement that comes in early June when the water is dropping off for the last time, and the early-run bright salmon are coming in from the sea. These fish seldom jump, but you know they are there. They are like ghosts in that regard. (You might hook one, at first mistaking it for a shad or a sea-run trout, until it heads out on its long run and it gives you that double-jump. Then you know it's a Rocky Brooker and that you will have your hands full for a long while. You holler for your brother or sister to come and give a hand with the landing.) The potato and the vegetable seeds have been put into the tilled fields, and you can smell this new-turned earth from the river.

A new pig has arrived (squealing) from a truck peddler, and the rooster chases a clucking hen across the dooryard to smother her with his flapping wings. From the garden, you can see that old river as it blinks through the trees against the bright sun and wind. The rhubarb leaves have become elephant ears. The scents of cut grass and hawthorn blossom blend with the pungent aroma of your parents' lilac trees. And there are petals of poplar and maple blossom drifting like confetti and purple caterpillars on the pollen-covered water. Toads sing all day and all night along the shores, and in the swamp, back of the cabin, there is a chorus of peeping young frogs, each trying to out-do the other as if it were a rite of spring.

The Miller Canoe is taken from the boathouse and painted; a new paddle is purchased. You go through your fly box to see what favourite patterns are left from last summer, remembering that your Shady Lady—tied by Blackville's Cathy Colford—was lost when you broke a leader up at Burnt Hill in August.

You get dressed in your khaki shirt and go to the same river where you caught your first bright salmon in June of '51. You throw the same cast over the same old rock where that first salmon is still present in your mind because you know that divining the territory and visualizing the take—as in a golf shot—is one of the most important fundamentals in fly-fishing. There is always a salmon waiting for you in a place like that; real or imagined, it carries the same anticipation. And you cast and enjoy the surroundings for the ten-thousandth time, while waiting for that fish to make its move and take you with it again, on its long run downstream as it leaps and capers against the strain of the line, which has a belly because the fish has suddenly swung and is heading back to you, just like the first salmon did so many decades ago. All fish are imitations of that first one caught. They are like lovers in that regard.

You fish through the yard-raking and the seed-planting days, the prom season, the weddings time of year, the church confirmation classes, the first communions, the river baptisms, the wakes, and the rituals when the old men set on the shores under lean-tos, smoke pipes and watch the ten-fathom gaspereau nets as their floats bob under from the weight of the fish. In a small stream back on the flat, they fillet their catches until their barrels are filled.

You fish through the warm-spell haying time, when the barn doors are propped open and there is seed drifting on the water like insect hatches. You fish into the dog days of August when the leaves of the current bushes are woolly and deep-veined; the salmon runs follow one after another, like someone has cranked up the migratory clock. And you fish into the harvest season, when the mornings are frosty and those flame-coloured fields of stubble glisten under the rising sun.

On occasion, you give a piece of fresh salmon to Uncle Dan's Ellen, who is now over ninety years old and still living alone in her farmhouse and cooking her own meals. (Ellen died of a heart attack three years ago and was brought back to life by doctors, giving a whole new meaning to the phrase "after years.") There is a slice for Uncle Jim's Annie, who is living with her daughter, Annie's Annie, and *her* daughter Annie, who is still in school. Annie's Annie married a

Mackenzie (an upriver name) from The Forks, but it did not work out. She is back at home with her mother, battling cancer and winning. There is a small piece for Aunt Maggie, widowed and living at home with her daughter since Father's half-brother, Jack, died. And there is a salmon steak for Burton, your second cousin by marriage. Yes, these pieces of fish will be delivered on paper plates from the seat of the truck so they can be fried for supper on the wood stoves of lamp-lighted summer kitchens.

There will be talk of these gifts after Mass at Holy Trinity Anglican Church in Blackville and Our Lady of Mount Carmel in Howard on Sunday mornings.

There is no need to explain away those September mornings when there is frost on the truck's windshield, and the scent of coffee is strong anywhere near the camp yard. You stand and smoke in the cold morning air, waiting for the woman you are guiding to finish her breakfast so that together you can head up along the shore to the Half Bar or the Johnston Rock Pool. Your friend has been here a dozen times, and without asking her, you know that is where she wants to go because that is where she caught her first big salmon on this very day, fifteen years ago. The fisher is a brain surgeon from Kansas City, and you are her river guide. But you have become friends for life — calling and emailing one another weekly — even though you live so many miles apart, because these same feelings are shared and relived time and again in fish caught and in the pursuit of fish. If you explain these things too often, especially to a non-river person, they cease to exist.

But if asked why you live here, you would just say that it is because you were born here and love this old place.

Fishing the High Country

I am wading downstream with a gentle breeze at my back and the sun strong against the collar of my cotton shirt. I am making the short casts into the dents of the big submerged rocks and my Grey Ghost—on the six-pound test leader—is tracking deep and straight across the dark, foam-beaded riffles. There are no clouds in the sky, but there had been rain in the night. And against the noonday sunlight, the undergrowth is silver with beaded drops, the river having risen slightly. I know it will run off quickly as I am far up in the head-waters of the Renous River system. I am fishing in those nameless little pools from where the salmon move quickly when the river is on the rise. I know there are fish in here, and I feel that when the sun drops behind the hills, they can be taken with the right fly hook and swing, although I am regretting not having brought the mosquito repellent.

I had hooked fish here in the seventies when the stream was filled with salmon that seemed to strike at my fly hook out of bravado. In the fast water they plopped on the surface—like when you throw in an egg-sized rock—before getting to the hook. These were the heavy-shouldered, early-run salmon that, when hooked, made the reel sing in high notes as they jumped a good three feet out of the water, and I had to reel fast to pick up the slack before the fish upended again and shook the hook free. But there was not much I could do to keep them away from the driftwood that had lodged in eddies and the big rocks that stood everywhere in the river like haycocks in a field. I had lost many fish, some through broken hooks and leaders. For sure, it was not an easy place to wade, and an even harder place to bring in a salmon.

Carl Manderville Sr., who was fishing ahead of me on that day in the seventies, appeared to be more interested in catching the pan-sized speckled trout that hung out in the bends in the shade of big sweeps. In June, these sea-run brookies would take a match-of-the-hatch if presented properly. For fifty years, Carl had been an outfitter and a guide on the Renous River and its branches, which include the Dungarvon and its tributaries, North and South Branch, along with the North and South Branch of Renous and North Renous Lake — and he knew these headwaters like a farmer knows his fields.

Carl's outfit, the Manderville farm, located on the South Renous Road, was at one time owned by Kingsbury Brown, who had purchased it from the Manderville people and who also owned a camp further upstream at the Bell Pool. As well, Brown owned an outfit of camps at Six Mile Brook on Cains River built by Carl. Carl Manderville was also a camp builder. In the early fifties, with his son Donald (then just a boy), they had built these log camps for Mr. Brown. Later, Brown sold the farm and properties to Charles W. Engelhard of Engelhard Industries in New Jersey, a group that also had a camp lease on North Renous Lake and a lodge there. The Bell Pool property was sold to Bill Connors, the fish warden/outfitter from Pineville, its log cabin having been destroyed by an ice jam in the winter of '73. By the time we fished together, Carl was operating the Manderville farm for Engelhard.

I am told that the Renous Engelhard properties had afterwards been sold to F.C. ("Buck") Dumaine Jr., the Boston railroad tycoon who for many years had been an owner of the Burnt Hill Fishing Lodge on the Main Southwest Miramichi. It is said that Mr. Dumaine in turn gave the farm to his son Dudley as a birthday gift. The Manderville farmstead has since been purchased by Andrew Dawson, a local man who has done some groundwork with plans to build a home there.

⌒

The North Branch of the Renous—this river—is really the outlet of North Renous Lake. The South Branch of the Renous heads up in the Guagus, or Guagus Lake. Of course the branches of the Dungarvon—both small, bony streams—are closed to angling for four miles below the Plaster Rock Renous Highway (Highway 108), where there is a counting fence. And on the Dungarvon Road, the main stream of the Dungarvon was and still is closed to all angling above the Furlong Bridge on September 15. These conservation measures, along with some stocking programs, are a part of the Renous River enhancement program, an affiliate of the Miramichi Salmon Association and the Atlantic Salmon Federation.

Having fished The Falls, The Gravel Pit, The Rocks, Moose Landing, and The Ledges, Carl and I were at the Sawdust Pool on the North Branch, where the river bends near the Red Bridge and where a lumber mill had been in earlier times. From here, the Forks Pool, where the North and South Branches meet, is a short drive and then a hike from the highway. At that time in the early seventies—after federal fisheries minister Roméo LeBlanc implemented a ban on all commercial fisheries in the Miramichi estuary—there was a salmon holding behind every rock on this river system, according to Carl. This network of little rivers is still consistent in its catches and has always been among the best producing salmon waters of the Miramichi drainage system.

This was beautiful country. Beyond the gravel shores and the over-hanging sod embankments, the forest floor was covered with pale new grass and knee-high ferns, pea green and fan-like on their transparent stems, the giant, whispering pine trees making broken shadows on the trails. And there were high, pine-covered hillsides—red, princess, and white pine—with their budding new growth that resembled so many candles set in decorative plaster of Paris holders. The big grey tree trunks leaned over the water that was tinted amber as it rushed past, and gave the rocky bottom an orange appearance, especially in the sharp bends where the water was deeper and a bit of grey driftwood had gathered on the surface because of the rise.

I found that seeing the place for the first time, feeling a sense of mystery about its past and feeling the risk of maybe never seeing it again actually served to enhance the landscape. In my mind, I sketched together a make-believe history, with old-world fishing scenes, woodsmen working the river drives, great horses and carriages on the move. I suppose my imagination was set on fire by the desire I had for something I knew I could not possess. A river is always moving, so that we never see the same one twice; the sky's colour, the breeze, the air's moisture add to the tapestry.

Everything here spoke to me, especially when the wind picked up to set the tall bracken moving in waves, which made the water a dark blue. I dreamed of building a log cabin—complete with a stone fireplace—overlooking this turbulent stream from the top of one of these pine tree bluffs. The moss-covered mounds were still here too, long knolls that Carl said were giant trees that had been destroyed by the Great Miramichi Fire of 1825. Others were hemlock that had been chopped down for their bark, the trunks left to rot and their coverings taken to the tanneries of J.J. Miller in Millerton on the Main Southwest.

Kingfishers flew up the river and lighted on the tree limbs that reached over the water. After some time, they gave a cackle and moved to another tree, their wings flapping in spurts, then gliding to roost again. In some of those long, deep-water holes where the river bends, I could see salmon. They were facing into the currents, unaware, their tails stroking the water like white-wash brushes. They were camouflaged to the surroundings and almost invisible to the human eye, like bonefish in the Caribbean, except for their shadows on the stream bed. So I looked for the shadows. There was no room for a back cast. Instead, I roll-casted the fly hook right over their noses and got no response. Finally, I caught a par (baby salmon) and held it under water to take it off the hook. If you touch those delicate little fish with dry hands, they will die.

Carl was fishing with a six-foot Orvis split bamboo rod and a Hardy Perfect reel. I carried his suitcase-sized fly box that was stuffed with leaders and hooks and reels for both trout and salmon. With the small rod, he was side-casting trout flies under the overhanging sods and near the roots of the trees that leaned over the water. I was fishing with my old eight-foot, ten-inch fibreglass Fenwick rod that weighed five ounces, and a number ten, double taper line on a four-inch St. John Hardy reel, which would be overkill on any stream by today's standards.

In my grandfather's day, while operating a lumber camp on the North Branch of Renous, Papa speared his fish at the Salmon Hole on the Dungarvon to supply the camp with salt salmon. At the upper end of the Salmon Hole, the fish rested with their heads in the shade of the big rock. At night, he stood on the rock and filled the salt barrel, which was transported to camp by his truck-wagon and matched team of strawberry roan horses, Muggins and Maud. With their tails and manes braided and tasselled, they pranced, lifting their feet high like soldiers marking time, or perhaps like the Arabian horses we see in bullrings, as if it were a ritual practised only in bringing salmon home. Those fish had been easy to spear, even in the deep water. There had been an old cabin on the hill where Papa slept and fed his horses between fishing hours. Remnants of that cabin and horse stable were still there in the early 1970s.

Salmon are harder to catch on a fly hook, and it takes special technique to fish a small stream like the North or South Branch Renous or the upper reaches of the Dungarvon. It is like fishing a big river, except everything is condensed to miniature proportions: the cast, the swing, the new reach presentation that may be reduced to just a few inches because the fish want it right on the nose. This is a series of little rivers with angling techniques that are not unlike the brown trout streams I have fished in New England, except they are more turbulent, with more ledges and giant trees.

The sun that had hammered down on the water all morning and afternoon—and had then moved to the hillsides, leaving long shadows that stretched across the water, and then to the treetops—had now disappeared from sight. I caught a small salmon in the Bridge Pool and released it after Carl told me to try a Shady Lady at seven o'clock sharp, the old witching hour.

Carl caught four pan-sized trout that, as he predicted, started to plop for a hatch after the sun went behind the hills. He cleaned the trout in a small stream, wrapped them with wet fern leaves, and tossed the entrails into the trees. These trout would be for the next morning's breakfast with fried eggs and pancakes at Carl's home in Bryenton.

Later in the evening, we stopped at the Half Way Inn. This place was stationed midway along the ninety-mile stretch of Highway 108, between the little community of Renous and the village of Plaster Rock, which are on opposite sides of New Brunswick. The chip seal road crossed all four of the tributary branches. In front of the inn, a frayed Canadian flag was flapping in the wind and we could hear coyotes howl. In the trees, many birds were singing, the smallest of them making the greatest sounds.

We took off our waders and sat on a bench to share a single malt

Scotch, because we knew there was no bar inside. Carl lit up one of his big Havana cigars, creating smoke to ward off the mosquitoes. So we drank the Manderville Scotch and inhaled the Cohiba cigar smoke, our faces feeling the scald of sunburn and fly bite. In the sand in front of us there was a moose track that looked like the ace of hearts.

Inside, we ordered a meal of boiled salmon — that day's special — which was served up with half-grown new potatoes, buttered carrots, and vinegar-sprinkled fiddleheads by innkeepers Sonny and Lois Hare. Sonny had been a police officer in the New Brunswick Highway Patrol and had retired to operate the inn. He was a big man who wore a ten-gallon hat, white T-shirt, and blue jeans. (From a distance, he looked like Hugh O'Brien's version of Wyatt Earp. For sure, he was a man from the gun generation when the western movies were all the rage.) When Lois came with the homemade blueberry pie and ice cream dessert, she smiled and asked if we had had any luck on the rivers. She told us that many anglers came to the restaurant each evening, hungry and tired after fishing in those hard-to-wade headwaters. She said that most of them wanted a good square meal and a chance to enjoy the hustle and bustle of the inn life after a lonely day on the water. Some stayed the night in adjacent cabins that were for rent.

There was an old upright piano against the panelled wall, so I sat down on the bench and hit a few wild chords to find out it was badly in need of tuning. I could not play the instrument anyway and, stopping my attempt, closed the cover just as people were gathering around me with their drinks to croon. One man started to sing, "Show me the way to go home, I'm tired and I want to go to bed." I have always found that people who fish, especially those who stay at inns, are looking to party when evening arrives. Maybe that is why I liked to stay at such places, though my wife detested them.

There was a brief thundershower with driving rain and high winds that made the doors of the inn bang and the chimneys creak and moan. Lightning flashed through the unshuttered windows for a split second of hyperborean reflection, lighting up the room to make us all look transparent, like a deer's eyes we see in car headlights. Thunderous rumbling, like oil drums rolling on the roof, contributed to the excitement of the moment. Carl said that this thunderstorm would kill the moose flies and horseflies. We never lost our power supply because the place, so far into the hills, was operating on a gasoline generator.

Carl and I thought about staying overnight, getting Lois to pack a lunch for us, and then fishing that lower stretch in the early morning, but we figured that our wonderful wives back in Bryenton and Millerton would be concerned. Carl was having some heart trouble by then, and of course, we had no cellphones in those days.

We started our homeward drive in the fading twilight, with the moon pushing over the northern horizon, the inky thundercloud growling in the south, and chains of lightning flashing down toward the treetops. From the crest of those high ridges, we could see for a hundred miles, the dark green of the spruce and pine trees contrasting with the pea green new-leafed poplar and birch. The chip seal highway, straight as an arrow, cut through them, with here and there a pale stream of blue or white smoke rising above the highest summits. Those big valleys indicated the course of some unseen waterways, the illusions that come with a place as yet undiscovered.

On the top of one summit, we came upon a tent trailer completely engulfed in flame. The blaze was leaping from its metal base, sending embers and cinders to the heavens, and there was a strong smell of burning canvas, plastic, and rubber. The smoke billowed straight up into the unfathomable sky. The trailer had been abandoned and was sitting on the side of the highway, its owners obviously having gone for help. We felt the heat as we drove past it, so close. Further out the road, we came upon the New Brunswick forestry service fire truck

(McGraw Brook Division), its sirens whining as it headed to the rescue with some cars following.

My big station wagon rolled along with only the rumble of the tires audible, the fire having caused a moment of reflection within Carl and me. We passed the McGraw Brook Ranger Station across from where, in my teen years, there had been a picnic site for prom parties and high school graduations. I could remember being there into the late night with a girlfriend from Blackville who had wooed me from long range on the school grounds. For a brief moment, not from the place but from somewhere within myself, I recaptured the person that I once was. Then like a lightning flash, it was gone and things were back to normal.

Soon Carl and I were on the banks of the main Renous River, passing the old Colepaugh place. This big, grey-shingled farmhouse had been a halfway inn for woods workers and caribou hunters in my grandfather's time, but had long since been abandoned, the upstairs windows busted out, their gauze curtains blowing like flags of surrender. In the dampness, we could smell the pungent lilac blossoms from the front garden, see the raindrops that were clinging to the spider webs on the iron gate.

We came down toward Pineville, passing the Blueberry Plains Road, the old Johnston place, and Flat Landing's salmon pool, which was fringed with beautiful elm trees, and then climbed Devils Back hill, travelling on down to where the woods turned into farmlands.

We drove slowly through the upper settlements and past what had once been the Pineville (covered) Bridge. The rainwater on the road glistened, and there were small ponds that the tires splashed over. Going through the little community of Renous, we could see the Manderville farm across the river, with its stately old farmhouse and hip-roof barn, its steel covering on fire now in the post-sunset. (I could remember having seen a moose hanging in the open doors of that barn the previous fall when Carl had a three-day licence. He and his nephew Kingsbury Manderville had shot the animal in that moose country across the Renous River from the McGraw Brook Ranger Station, where Freeman MacDonald was then head warden.) The little houses along the road were purple with coppered windows, and above the ditches the glistening brass power lines sagged between the poles. In pastures, under the big shade trees, black-and-white cows lay contentedly, a sense of peace and quietness about them. Then we could hear the bell tolling at Saint Bridget's Roman Catholic Church, see groups of older people wandering along to Mass that we knew would be administered by the local priest, Father Vincent Donovan, the river's patriarch whose home we had just passed. The big stone church shifted its position, and indeed its spirit, in sequence to our passing car.

Having driven past the ivy-clad abutments of the railway overpass, soon we were at the mouth of the Renous River and cruising along the Main Southwest Miramichi, leaving behind wayside farms with their old grey barns and pastures, where the tilled land and pistil apple orchards brought the fields to life. The railway tracks ran parallel to Highway 108, with the winking red signal lamps forewarning the long-armed crossings at Upper Derby and Bryenton. I could sense the ghost of the province's most famous train, the Dungarvon Whooper, long out of commission by then.

Below the Quarryville Bridge, the river was big and flat and slow-moving as a lake while it ebbed with the tides, and we could see the bushed-over boom blocks at angles across the water. These had been left in place from the log-rafting years, when the saw mills in Millerton and Newcastle had sent the rough-sawed planking to the yards that built the tall ships. There was a lumber boom here in the mid-nineteenth century when deal and planks were sent overseas by sail. Some of the stately homes in Millerton were built in that day, as was the brick-coloured clapboard train station in Millerton, a part of the Snowball Gibson Railway Line, which was built by those two lumber lords, the railway's namesakes, in 1886 and dismantled in 1986. We drove on toward my little farmhouse, with its awning-drooped windows and green wood shutters, that I had jokingly named Wayside after visiting Nathaniel Hawthorne's home in Concord, Massachusetts.

Indeed, it was one of those suspended country moments: a magnificent twilight drive in an atmosphere that happens once in a lifetime. It was that kind of sacred evening, which only William Wordsworth could have put into adequate words. I always had a tendency toward melancholy and, yes, solitude, a condition I have no desire to discard. But during that drive, there was a state of mind I was never able to recapture, though I drove that road a hundred times since. Maybe it was my youthful imagination, enhanced by a big meal—I had a great appetite in those days—or the single malt, and a tired body. But I believe that youth is when our impressions are strongest. In later years, I would look upon such an evening's drive in a more practical way, with the notion that the landscape is eternal and speaks to everyone with the same voice.

⌣

Carl Manderville and I had planned on going back to the upper branches of Renous to test those pools further downstream, below The Forks. We wanted to get into the water at The Ledges and wade down that bigger river to the "take-out" place where a four-wheel-drive truck would be waiting for us. We also planned to go—with our families—to North Renous Lake for a day's fishing and maintenance work, and then have a party in the lodge, where we would spend the night. Carl also wanted to canoe with me down the Main Southwest Miramichi, through the Gray and White Rapids—dangerous water—from Blackville to Quarryville.

But on May 3 in the spring of '76, Carl Manderville took a heart attack at his home in Bryenton, and died three days later in the Miramichi Hospital.

Since then, the old Manderville farmhouse — as we knew it — has burnt to the ground, as has the cookhouse, barn, and the big lodge on North Renous Lake. Only the canoes were salvaged from the fire, and they were stacked on a trailer and brought by his sons to Carl's farm in Bryenton.

Today the Half Way Inn sits idle and is in much need of repair. Sonny Hare is long dead. But the salmon run remains healthy in crystal waters that have flowed through those hills for a zillion years.

I still think of Carl when I come here to fish. I can smell, even taste, the fragrance of his Cuban cigar, feel the muscle strain of carrying his box of flies, slipping on the pine needles, from pool to pool along those rocky shores. He had lived and worked here so long that his spirit is steeped into the land and river, which, to me, is very near to God. For sure, it was a time to be relived through the magic of metaphor, the natural image of river and hill. These images keep it strong even now, so many decades later, as I work my way downstream below The Forks.

The Distant Lakes Are Calling

On the first of May, opening day for the trout angling season, my friend Johnny Carnahan and I loaded his fibreglass canoe onto the roof of my station wagon and set out for Buck Horn Lake. From Millerton, it was a half-hour Sunday drive up the chip seal Plaster Rock Renous Highway, turning off on the Fraser Burchill Road, from where we swung onto a winding gravel byway that led up a long hill. We passed Lucky Gray's deer-hunting camp and went on into heavy woods where, at the top of a big hill, we got a glimpse of the lake. It gleamed like a stainless steel plate under the morning sunlight.

We had driven to a bluff from where we were looking right down on the compound, which had patches of snow beneath the black spruce and leafless maple trees along its shores. Up there in the high country, it was cold from the northwest breeze that made the trees toss about and the water sparkle. It cut through our spring coats and hats and made us shiver. On the sunny hillside, the birch trees were budding, and there were mayflowers that we stopped to admire, even taste—a great treat after a cruel winter—but in the shade of trees, the winter's chill was as present as the ghost of old church disciplines.

We did not attempt to drive over the hill; rather, we unloaded the boat at the parking area and put our tackle and lunches into the canoe's belly, dragging the whole concern down a converging path, over patches of grey moss and old snow to the murmuring, rough water's edge.

With Johnny seated in the bow, we set out to make our way toward the inlet, which was on the far side of the lake. The way it is with lakes, this one did not look so big from where we had parked the car, but when we got out on the water's surface, we realized it was huge. Sitting in the stern, I found it was hard canoeing against the choppy water, our paddles bumping against the gunwales as we tried to reach down deep. The wind made the cold spray from under the chin of the boat and the drip from Johnny's paddle splash against my face. His old hat blew off, and we let it drift away and sink. We had to be careful to steer squarely into the wind because we knew if we got crosswise in those big, rolling swells, the little sixteen-foot Old Town could capsize. And, of course, we could not swim, nor did we wear life jackets in those days.

I could remember having come here with my uncle Wilfred during my schooldays, and after spending long hours on the lake without seeing any fish, I went back to his car to read. The old man was surprised that a boy living in the country, where there was so much outdoor activity, could be a reader.

"Lord God almighty!" he swore. "What is wrong with your head?" (Wilfred was a comical old man who knew the ways of the rivers and lakes. I recall once at a dinner party at our house, he attempted to show the other guests how to get back into a canoe if it capsized on a lake. When he finished telling the story, he was on his knees on top of the cupboard.)

In truth, that experience with Uncle Wilfred was my first on a lake of any size, and I was disappointed. I had pictured it like a pond I had read about in my school reader, where there had been a campfire and a white canvas tent and an owl roosting in the branches of a tall pine tree. In the school pictures, there had also been deep reflections of the trees — and the fire blinking at the water's edge — in the clear, smooth compound. But here at Buck Horn, the wind was stinging cold, the water rough, with no campfire and no tent in which to warm ourselves.

This was the lake where, shortly after that trip with my uncle, the Matchett brothers, Benny and Guy—from Williamstown, New Brunswick—drowned in the spring of '58. Their small craft capsized, and they got tangled in the fishing lines and the anchor rope that dragged them under. Their bodies were found by Mounties a few days later. With these young men having come from a place so handy to our homes, I have had a fear of lakes ever since. Still, the lure of the wilderness, combined with being the first ones to fish the gorgeous water after the long cold winter, made Johnny and I pumped to go.

McKendrick Lake was not far up the road, and it was totally reachable by car. Indeed, there was a big government-owned cabin at the water's edge that had later been used as a children's Bible camp. While that more accessible lake was stocked with trout, we had heard rumours that it had been fished hard by the camp students and the Baptist minister. So we opted for Buck Horn.

This was my second real experience in lake fishing, as I had grown up on a river and knew the ways of the moving stream: how the water was going in one direction and how to navigate this flow against wind, rain, or snow—and, if necessary, all of the above at once. If I capsized, there were ways to cling to the boat and, with the help of the moving water, work my way to shore by touching bottom here and there, letting the water push me into a bend close enough that I could grab the bushes and haul myself onto dry land. Of course, on either lake or river, if anyone capsizes this early in the spring, they have to move fast and get out of the water that is just one or two degrees above freezing. You have about four minutes, they say, to navigate your own survival.

But, unlike a river, a lake has no moving water and no sure bottom. Up in those hills, at that time of year, the wind picks up in seconds, and you find yourself facing six-foot-high swells. It takes all the canoe savvy anyone might have to swing that small craft around in the cross-chop and paddle for dear life against the wind—with your hands numb on the paddle and the froth hitting your face that is red from the cold—to get safely back to the launch area.

This day with Johnny, however, the waves were not so high and we paddled across Buck Horn to the inlet and dropped the anchor about fifteen feet from shore. We cast out flies into the turbulent waters of the incoming stream, which appeared to be about ten feet wide and was fast-moving with the spring runoff. We were a solitary canoe, tossing about on the waves of this beautiful lake on the first day of the season. I was fishing with the semi-dry fly hook Rat Faced McDougal, casting it into the running stream and letting it drift out into the purple waters, which against the morning sunlight looked biblical in the shadows, and like they should have been the home of some big speckled trout. But we saw nothing except the bottom-feeding suckers that were as big as grilse and that I did not know inhabited the lakes. Johnny was using a streamer he called the Black Ghost.

Casting away, we both became thoughtful and sat for a long time without saying a word. We were enjoying the setting, which could have been a high-resolution photo out of a *Field & Stream* magazine, or perhaps John and Janet Foster's television show, *To the Wild Country*. For a time there was great unrest among the crows—a dozen or more—and I wondered if we had invaded their nesting territory. But then behind us, high in the branches of a double white pine tree, I saw an eagle. In profile, it looked like a sketch of an owl one might see in a child's Halloween colouring book. I thought, The pine trees have a good spirit about them.

I have always thought of such places as sanctuaries, even monasteries: places in which to meditate, find God. Nature in all seasons has a beauty all its own. I had given myself up to such pleasant thoughts, long past the current day's experiences, and was somewhere in the long summer that lay ahead. Sunday is a good day for meditation. Johnny was also in a trance, sitting silently in his habitual repose, sucking on his rattling old pipe, the smoke of which drifted past me in whiffs. With his bare head and straight-stemmed pipe, he looked like my boyhood radio and comic book hero, Mark Trail. I always enjoyed the company of older people: Johnny was twenty-odd years my senior.

For me, there were two lakes here: the one I was fishing and the one that I had been dreaming about coming to since last winter. I tried hard to stay in the imagined one because there had been big trout in it. The school-book photographs, I had realized, were works of art and not realistic—not in this high country.

After about an hour of trying different fly patterns and presentations, we decided that while Buck Horn was pretty, and indeed dreamy and spiritual, it seemed fishless. Maybe we should go to another lake. We had heard stories about lake fishing and that it was important to get to these places as soon as possible after the ice left them. This was obviously not the case on Buck Horn. (I now believe it is more about the timing and being lucky enough to catch the trout-feeding frenzies that chase after the insect hatches.)

We paddled back across the lake with the wind at our backs, and as we neared the shore, we could see on the hill the chrome bumpers of my white station wagon as they glistened in the hot inland sun. At the launch area we got out of the canoe and stood and smoked cigarettes —Lucky Strike for good luck, or so we thought. We disassembled our tackle and were getting ready to drag the canoe back up the hill when I noticed, not thirty feet from the water's edge, some fish were rolling up and splashing about, as if to pick something off the surface. We watched for a few minutes, then we reassembled our rods and reels and started casting from the shore, wading into the shallow areas to the top of our rubber boots.

I was using a Jack Sullivan–tied Ingalls Butterfly with white goat-hair wings (dyed yellow) and a red tip. This salmon fly was designed for slow or dead water. And as I cast well out and brought the fly forward in small jerks — like a water bug in distress — I started to get hits, even strikes. In the course of the next half-hour, I hooked five trout, all of which weighed in the half-pound category. Johnny was doing the same and had caught one that weighed over a pound. We caught our limit of five, dragged the boat back up the hill, loaded it onto the car, and drove back to our home community, with the understanding that we need not have left the lakeshore or taken the canoe. It was, indeed, just a question of knowing the species and their ways.

And I wondered at the time, if we had stayed at the inlet on the far side of the lake, if we would have got bigger fish. But that is the way it is with trout fishing: you can fish for a long stretch and not see anything, or have on the wrong fly pattern. And then, suddenly from below, a certain hatch will unearth itself and come to the surface. The lake will come to life with action, and if you happen to be there at the right time and are able to match the hatch, you will have some luck, as Johnny and I did that morning.

I remember once on North Renous Lake, it was summer, and I was fishing with Russell Manderville, my ex-wife's uncle, and his brother-in-law Charles Gatley, a landscape artist from Dedham, Massachusetts. (Russell had been born here but had moved to the United States as a young man and was home on a holiday.) We were staying at the Engelhard camp, a large cabin with fireplace, big log walls, a lot of old-world charm, and, as I recall, old-world plumbing. But things are always smaller than they appear in memory. Carl Manderville — also a relation of my ex-wife — was the caretaker and had given us the keys to the property. Upon arrival, we opened the windows in the perpetually bat-smelling rooms, had a drink of beer, and got rigged up to fish, dragging two canoes from the adjacent boathouse.

We were angling near the outlet, the North Branch of the Renous River, when the trout started to rise for a little green fly. We had only the one between us, so we took turns with the fly hook until the fish had mangled and ravelled it into shreds.

It was a hot day. We sat on the shore in the shade of trees and con-templated our next move. Thinking we would do some real business if we had more green flies, we came back out to the Miramichi River and then drove to Doaktown—a good forty miles—and to W.W. Doak's tackle shop, where we purchased a dozen green-feathered fly hooks.

The next day, we went back to the lake, travelling over those bumpy and dusty roads in two vehicles—we had brought Canadian Army veteran and outdoor photographer Burton Fowlie with us—and we started fishing the green flies. (Burton, dressed in khaki field clothing and a hard-shell jungle hat, from a distance looked like Colonel Flint.) We fished those flies at all different depths, different strokes, different angles, different areas of the lake, and at different times of the day, but we never got a rise. We guessed the hatch had changed to some other pattern or fly-hook simulation.

I remember that day. The lunch we had eaten in the old cabin consisted of a variety of cheeses and breads and some good wines that Charles Gatley had brought from Boston. Afterwards, Fowlie lit a Churchillian cigar off the wick of the lamp. Sitting across from me at the table, he drank coffee as he showed us photographs of the days when he was a company commander in the Canadian Armed Forces during the Second World War. He had served in England, Belgium, and France. One picture was of him in uniform, standing next to actor Clark Gable (by then considered the "King of Hollywood"), who was a rear gunner and a first lieutenant in the United States Air Force. The two men had met in the fall of '42 in Presque Isle, Maine, when Fowlie was training in Edmundston, New Brunswick: the two camps were about eighty miles apart.

For the Americans, Presque Isle was the nearest airfield from which they could fly the B-17 bombers to Europe. It was then that the photograph was taken, not long after the movie *Gone with the Wind* had premiered on the big screen in Atlanta—and according to Fowlie, for privacy, Clark Gable did most of his studying in toilets. Accompanying Gable was MGM cameraman Andrew McIntyre, who was to do a propaganda film for the military featuring Gable to entice enlistment in the United States Air Force. Burton told us that he had driven across the border many times to visit Clark Gable, who was there for three weeks. This made for good conversation here at the cabin.

After lunch, Fowlie set up a tripod on the floor of the veranda and viewed the big lake and hills through a telescope while the rest of us fished. He was focused on some distant ponds and beds of reeds that swayed in the currents near the far shore, where black spruce treetops pierced the azure sky. I believe he was more interested in photographing scenery and wildlife—perhaps a moose that might wander into the lake, perhaps a great blue heron, perhaps the dark shadow of a tree that reflected upon the water—than catching trout or salmon.

Yes, there were salmon in North Renous Lake too, having come in the outlet that fed the North Branch of the Renous River. Carl Manderville told me that he once caught a black salmon there on July 12, the fish having been landlocked since the spring runoff. But that trip to North Renous Lake was a learning experience for us all. We had great conversation about the old days and the future. We talked about fish caught, and we relived some of the times we had shared in the pursuit of fish and a higher quality of life.

The Distant Lakes Are Calling

In the late seventies, George Johnston was operating a fishing outfit on Long Lake and Island Lake, which are about thirty miles from Plaster Rock, New Brunswick. (George was from Plaster Rock too.) He had built a number of cozy cabins, some of logs and some of drop siding, overlooking Long Lake—which also had a rocky island in view of the camp where he kept anglers, and in the fall, deer hunters. He had invited me to come to stay a few days and maybe do a story on the operation because he needed the press. Back then, I had been doing some writing for Tourism New Brunswick.

So on the long weekend in May, I loaded up my Jeep and drove there from our cabin in Keenan with my wife, Janet Manderville, along with my three sons, Jeff, Jason, and Steven. It was an eighty-mile journey on dusty gravel roads.

George welcomed us by lighting the propane lamps and making a fire in the big iron, glass-door stove that was in the main cabin. We seemed to be the only people in camp on that long weekend. Again, in that high country, there were lingering patches of snow in the woods around the lake.

I could remember having gone on a bird hunt with Johnny Carnahan and his son Earl to Stewart Brook Lake for the Thanksgiving weekend in the fall of '69. It was beautiful country up there, with the small auburn lake surrounded by yellow reeds and orange aspens and the woods thereabouts filled with grouse, the forest floor speckled with deer tracks. But as I recall, it rained all weekend, and not having taken the proper rainwear, we mostly stayed in the camper, played cards, and ate big meals.

"It is not a fit weekend to leave a grindstone out of doors," John had joked.

But this trip, we did not fish the first day. Instead, a bush pilot and George took us for rides in the yellow Beaver, which had been landing on these lakes and others that George had leased from the New Brunswick government. It was docked in front of the cabins, and we stood on its pontoons to climb aboard.

The lakes had been stocked with togue, a lake trout that can grow as big as a salmon. (The largest known togue captured in North America was taken in a gill net in Lake Athabasca, Saskatchewan, on August 8, 1961, by Mr. Orton Flett. It weighed 102 pounds and was 49 inches in total length.)

The lakes, rough from the wind and ink stained, were beautiful from the sky, and we got a scope of just how big Long Lake really is. It is eleven miles from end to end, and with the sharp-faced, red cliffs on the north side, and with the dark green and grey woods, speckled with snow, it was an awesome sight. There were a few tiny boats out there bobbing about with people dressed in snowmobile suits, trolling their long, deep lines for the togue. In the distance, we could see Trouser Lake and Stewart Brook Lake and a hundred lesser lakes whose names I no longer remember. In the far hills, there was the serpentine region and the narrow, black Tobique River with a few hamlets along its shores, then the cliffs of Mount Carleton.

The water in Long Lake that day was rough with white-capped breakers, and when the pilot circled low and the little plane, which seemed to be held together with Scotch tape, set down into these six-foot swells, I felt we would all perish for sure.

The pilot crossed himself, which was not a confidence builder.

My wife, who was afraid but not crying, said, "Boys, this is it. We'll never see the mouth of the Cains River again."

I was more afraid of running out of fuel, as the gas gauge appeared to be showing empty. Through the morning, the bush pilot had been taking the young women from the cook camp on joy rides, circling the lake and motoring up to the small dock where there was a lot of laughter and whooping.

Nauseated from the altitude change and the turbulence, we went back to our cabin for a Gravol pill but with new-found wonderment about the beautiful scenery here in our home province, the peacefulness of lakes and the dark-treed mountains.

In New Brunswick, the deepest and best producing compounds for togue are lakes such as Long Lake, Chamcook Lake, and Grand Lake. While many smaller lakes support fewer numbers, these waters probably hold the best populations throughout the Atlantic region. George told us that the togue stay in the extreme depths and have to be trolled for with spinners and spoons, something I had never done before and really knew nothing about. He said that these fish are known to inhabit the waters from the northernmost top of the Yukon and Alaska through the Atlantic provinces of New Brunswick and Nova Scotia. They are native fish of these landlocked, underwater worlds, and since the beginning of time, masters of their kingdom.

I came to realize that for the angler seeking high adventure, the quest for this game fish could provide a great challenge. George said that careful strategies were rewarded with the thrill of a fierce battle and, probably, capture. Of course, we were prepared to release all of our catches.

The best time for angling the togue is in the early spring, immediately after the ice melts away. They are known to mill about in the cool water, near the surface, before the water begins to warm from the sun. Later they move to the extreme depths, keeping below the warm water level during the summer months, where they feed on white fish and other trout fingerlings of their own species. According to documents I read at the cabin, during the early spring and late autumn, when they have moved to the shallows, they live on suckers and chubs as well as insect hatches.

The next morning, we were up early and had breakfast at the long plank table in the dining-room end of the main cabin. The lodge was big enough to sleep and feed twenty people, so there was plenty of room at the table. George had come into the kitchen at daybreak to build up the fires. After breakfast, we bundled up and made preparations to go out onto the lake. Janet decided to stay in camp as she had twisted her ankle when she jumped down from the pontoon onto the dock after the airplane landed the day before. She kept three-year-old Steven with her. Jeff, Jason, and I got into George's big metal boat.

He pushed us off with the words, "If the motor shuts off or if yuz run out of gas, I will pay for the repairs, but if yuz strike a rock and break a prop or a cut off a pin, it is your responsibility."

Fair enough.

We motored out into the big lake a few hundred yards, and then I cut the motor to a crawl and we threw our hardware over the side to troll, long and deep as instructed. We were using the string of silver spoons on a swivel and a heavy twenty-pound test leader that George had given us. We trolled this way for an hour or so and got no strikes. When I noticed the wind picking up in the bigger part of the lake, we headed back in to shore. We were cold and hungry from exposure to the elements, which in that high country appeared to be well behind the calendar spring we had been enjoying back home. Plus, I had had a bad experience just a few years before, when I and two friends from North Bay, Ontario, were caught on Lake Ontario and spent an afternoon rowing and rowing in a desperate effort to get back to shore. We had been attempting to photograph some wild geese that were floating on the surface near Niagara-on-the-Lake. I have always been wary of big water after that traumatic experience.

When we returned to camp, there was a local man on the shore who had some lake trout in a creel, but he refused to let us photograph them.

"These are my fish," he said. "If you wanna take pictures, catch your own fish."

How silly, I thought. Photographs were to the advantage of promoting George Johnston and his outfitting business, not me. It did not occur to me until days later that the man's reluctance to have his fish photographed may have been because some of them were under the legal size for retention.

That evening for dinner we had barbecued salmon and good wine. George joined us and we ate in the living room while sitting in front of the piping hot, glass-fronted stove. George told us during the meal that at that time of spring, we should troll about a hundred yards from shore and use large spoons in a string about eighteen inches long that flash on a light wire (shock tipped) with live bait near the hook. We had used the wrong bait and a too-short leader. He said that as the season progressed into summer, other angling methods with depth-finders and fish-finders were necessary. George said that when a togue strikes, it quickly submerges to great depths and will never break water. In the big lakes where these fish survive, they most always run vertically instead of horizontally when hooked—unlike Atlantic salmon, which are leapers.

Some of the lakes in Atlantic Canada had been stocked. At that time, officials had released 3,400 prime broodstock fingerlings into Long Lake. There was a restriction that any trout caught under fourteen inches in length had to be released. It was then I realized why the man on shore had refused to let us photograph his fish. The angling record in North America was at that time 63 pounds, 2 ounces for a trout caught in Lake Superior in the spring of '52. In most inland lakes, however, the average weight was less than ten pounds.

George said that all the lakes of Atlantic Canada inhabited by the togue appeared to be untouched by airborne pollution, acid rain, or PCBs, and the fish remained edible. Many Northern Ontario lakes had already been ruined by the deadly acid, and the togue had vanished completely from those waters.

We enjoyed a beautiful dinner and great conversation with a man who had spent his lifetime in the outfitting business and knew the lakes so well. I was sorry I could not have spent more time with him before our little expedition ended. But I went to bed with a promise to myself that I would come back someday, and I would hire a local guide who knew the water, as I did the Miramichi River back home.

The next morning we awoke late. I looked out the window to see grey clouds hanging low over the black turbulent lake. The wind had picked up and it was snowing slantwise, the big wet flakes clinging to the trees and the gables of the adjacent cabins. But that is the way it is on a May day in the highlands: it can be sunny and warm at one hour, and then the sky darkens and you are seemingly right back in the middle of March. Yes, it had suddenly become a stormy winter morning.

We packed our luggage, bid farewell to our host, and started for home on gravel roads that were wet but still bare. While we drove, the snow turned to rain as we headed south and home to an environment that was more familiar to us. For we were river people, first and last, and had found the big lakes spooky, their waters angry in comparison to our home stream, even though the Miramichi River was also swollen and discoloured at that time of spring. But I guessed this comfort was more about where we had grown up than the quality of the waters that we knew so well.

On Reading the Water

Like an ancestral river person, a salmon stream's favours cannot be won over in one angling season, or even two or three. We are hard to get to know, and on the river, harder still to simulate as the river itself—its moods and its bounty—is in our minds. If you are from away, you might catch a salmon on your first time on the water, but more than likely it will be by accident or sheer luck. For the newcomers—hearing the stories on a bootleg basis, reading the books, seeing the films—the river is at first a novelty (especially if they have the good fortune of hooking a fish), then a fad, and then, depending on the depth of their commitment to it, an obsession.

To try to fit in, to really become one of us, all the scientific strategies are studied; these are books written mostly by other non-river people. (Tell me what you read, and I'll tell you who you are.) Much time is spent trying to become at one with our waters and their species. The best of canoes, wading boots, and tackles are purchased, and all the different conservation groups are joined. Their plastic stickers are pasted to car windows and on trailer doors—sure signs of an outsider. Fundraising dinners are attended, conservation awards are handed out to the big donors, and reputations are earned as great fly fishers, conservationists. Of course, this is all in the river's best interest, its economy and its reputation as a good salmon stream. And also to make a name for themselves as classic fly fishers, the acceptance of other would-be river people in the same circles is of great importance.

I have seen this happen a hundred times. In fact it has happened to me, more than once. And I was born and raised on the Miramichi, the mother of all salmon rivers. Unless we are born on the river, and live here full time, have guided for a living, and fished for the dinner table, it is easy for us to drift away from it, especially if the salmon runs have dropped off and the catch averages have declined. When this happens, the sameness of habit can reduce things to a silence. It takes a true river person to carry on, keep enthusiastic about the game in such cases. Yes, you coast away from it for a season or two, but then you find that you are missing the river's healing power. You come back to the river, once more, and with even greater enthusiasm.

Like a rediscovered old love, again you grasp the river's subtle spirit, the myth, the superiority of soul, the beckoning arms, for a summer, a season, or even a decade, and that is where all the trails lead you. Again. For a short time, a portion of your youth comes back to you. The fishing has been good, and on Facebook you see your own photographs: the bending rod, the leaping salmon, holding up a fish for the world to see.

When the salmon runs are less frequent and the fishing has tightened up, and suddenly the environmental extremists are talking about outright extinction of the species this time, you soldier on: casting away, waiting for that same big thrill of a taking fish, willing to release your catch. You realize that it is not about the fish but the fishing that you are here for, not about the love but the pursuit of love; this, and the circle you have become a part of, the crowd that thinks of you as a great fisherperson.

But then one day she—the river, I mean—goes away and stays. And you will find yourself on a golf course, taking lessons from a would-be club professional, shaking hands with people you do not know or care to know, trying to fit into the clique while caught up in a make-believe world of bright-coloured clothing, juvenile club politics (you are appointed games captain because of who you know), measured conversations, political correctness, social climbing, and of course, the meticulous etiquette—for hours, even days, on end. This has happened to me, and I am a deep-rooted river person. It was a weak period, I suppose, at a time in my life when I was a nervous wreck, brought on by the demands of the fast-moving city and years of monotonous factory life.

⌣⟶

When I first came home from Ontario, after having played golf for years in Niagara—it was my only escape there—I was caught between the two solitudes. I still wanted to golf, yet when I was on the golf course, I missed the river, which was so near to my place physically, mentally, and metaphorically, and was in fact the real reason I had moved back home: the great river and the quality of the air I was now breathing, the closeness to real nature. I wanted to fish, yet when I was on the river, I missed the golf course: the long drive off the tee, the birdie putt, the congratulatory applause from fellow golfers. Yet I found the rewards of golf, which should have been comparable to canoeing a rapid, to wading into the stream and hooking and playing a salmon—to be frivolous.

So I gave up golf. Now, I believe you can do both if you are living in the right location. Before my cabin was built, I was living in Millerton, within driving range of both river and golf course. In fact, I could see the river estuary from my farmhouse.

But your passion would not be totally committed to either one, and consequently, you would not do either one well. It would be like trying to be a good writer while playing violin in the symphony orchestra. These passions are both time-consuming and demand a person's full commitment.

In my case, the posterity—a big pull to the river, where I had spent so much of my boyhood, which was so much more relaxing and romantic — made the decision for me. One breezy June day, I was playing the fourth hole at the local club, and playing quite well for an amateur. But then, through the trees, I saw the sparkling water. On the river wind I could smell the dried algae on the rocks along the shores, hear the chuckle of boats, taste the fish-scented sparkle the sun was laying on the water, smell the life jackets and fish-scented scoop nets. And I never hit another golf ball to where I wanted it to go. Nor did I care. The river had beckoned and my golf game drifted into thin air.

You see, subconsciously, my thoughts had shifted to the old home stream and the salmon runs, to the boats and the rods and reels, and to the river cabins with their screened-in verandas and their wicker chairs that face the water. I could smell the smoke of my camp kitchen range; taste the frying bacon, the buckwheat pancakes, and brewing coffee; hear the singing of Hardy reels, the two-fold sounds of a jumping salmon on the line; see the sight of that old fly-tying bench where I had spent so many of my schooldays.

To me, this proved that the river is a harder-found but a longer-lasting romance, which is the way with all good romances. In the words of Marcel Proust, "The difference which exists between a person or a work of art that are markedly individual and the idea of beauty exists just as much between what they make us feel and the idea of love or of admiration." You almost have to be born on a river to feel, to fully comprehend, to really understand the river's ways, her disappointments and her rewards, and to live in her air and water space. Just as true mountain people, like farmers who dwell in the mountains of Switzerland, find a lack of proximity, a lack of understanding with mountain enthusiasts, would-be mountaineers, and mountain admirers who come to play on her slopes. It would be the same in England's Lake District where outdoor lovers, landscape writers, painters, and poets, wearing the long riding boots and shepherd's hats, get their pictures taken with a local shepherd and the attendant flock of sheep and dogs. They will never truly understand the shepherd's way of life. The shepherds will greet them kindly, stand for a photograph, but pass them off as outsiders who are oblivious to the lives they are living, and always will be.

But once you have become anointed with a river's water, once she gets into your bloodstream, as she did in mine at an early age, you can be around her longer and in the worst of conditions and still feel the passion. Because she has become a part of your soul. So that in your senior years, long after your knees and your long-distance eyesight have begun to fail, you go on loving her, most likely because she is, unlike a golf course, beyond the grasp of any one person to master—new- or old-comer alike—or to love solely as their own. Like a true love, a river is more remote, harder to attain, but once captured, harder to let go of. A river cannot be just selected to love because of her beauty or for the healing power she brings to us; rather, the pairing comes from the chemistry of having lived with her for years so that you have gotten to know her moods, her spirits, and she has become kin. Posterity makes this happen after a while—yes, even with a river.

As for those young or old who have no intimate connection whatsoever to the stream, no association with the mountains or lakes either, they are deaf and dumb to their ways. This passion is as unattainable and as meaningless as a dressmaker's dummy. You will probably be happier playing darts down at the Legion hall.

I believe that all rivers—William Faulkner's and Mark Twain's Mississippi, John Steinbeck's Salinas, Joseph Conrad's Congo—are for romantics.

Yet I do not consider my pull to the river to be a virtue, but rather a stigma, maybe even a handicap when it comes to dealing with society. There are so few of us and with no big common circle, no Sunday afternoon coverage on television, no mention in newspapers, no committees, and no wool sweater with a fraternity crest on the sleeve. Yet, like a beautiful sunset or a cloud formation, the river is there for all people who observe her and wish to get to know her intimately as a healer. The river is always moving, literally, and is never the same body of water for two seconds in a row. Yet she will love you back simply by being there when you need her, and because you have the sophistication to see her and admire her for what she really is. She is not a monogamous lover like a Canada goose; she is there for everyone who takes the interest to look deeply into her spirits and the myth born out of the heart, her ebbs and flows, and perhaps do a bit of meditation. You heal from the wounds of life that way, though I don't like that overused phrase.

As in golf and knowing the fundamentals required to play a decent round without embarrassment, fly-fishing can be a dull experience if you do not know, or care to know, the water and its ways, or if you are content merely to catch a fish once in a while, accidentally. Leaving the river spirits and meditations aside, a layman can spend hours, days, or even weeks angling a stretch of river with little to no success in catching a fish. You can consume a lot of time casting over the wrong areas that may appear "fishy" to the human eye, but are actually barren of aquatic life. Or you may angle over the so-called "hot spots" with the wrong casting slant and retrieve actions and, consequently, the wrong fly patterns. And if you do finally get a fish to strike, it's apt to shake itself free because it was hooked on a fly that was presented from the wrong side of the run, or perhaps just on a free-drifting slack line where there should have been a little swing, some hand action. When this happens, seasoned river people will look at you and chuckle, just as the well-informed golfer would do if you were trying to par a long golf hole by choosing the wrong club or putt a golf ball from out of a water hazard. As a kid fishing for the dinner table, I learned these things out of necessity, as did my brothers and my sister when we were just schoolchildren. All river youngsters learn these things as a matter of course, if not for the family's survival.

To the knowledgeable angler, there is no such thing as unfishable water. If you know the river, you know that salmon can be caught just about anywhere on a given day. But fish want fly hooks presented to them in natural ways. Some people never learn this. Instead, they blame their lack of success on the conditions, the equipment, the guide, bad luck, or even the environment. I have done all of this, while someone who actually knew what they were doing and knew the water's flow stepped into the pool behind me at the right time of day, with the right fly hook, the right cast angle and retrieve, and hooked and landed fish. They knew what they were doing because they had studied and knew the local water.

Blissfield outfitter Jack Sullivan used to say, "Knowing the water is the most important thing in the world: the water and the speed your fly hook needs to be travelling is everything."

In my sixty-odd years of salmon angling, I have learned that when fishing without a guide, one of the best ways to read never-before-fished water is to go downstream from the alleged holding areas, wade out, and look upriver from a position that is low to the water's surface. From this vantage point, you can see the water coming at you from many directions. This is especially effective in the early morning, before the sun hits the river, and there are patches of foam adrift. While this is not the best time of day to angle — the water temperatures are generally warmer than the air, and this contrast is always a factor — it is a good time to observe a given stretch of water, to see where its heaviest currents are, which indicates the angle of presentation required, the line's swing (that should not have a belly), the speed of retrieve, and so on. Your cast should be straight and at an angle, like the hands of a clock at ten past ten, and should swing from you like a pendulum on a grandfather's clock, without a curve or a wrinkle. When you do feel the pull of a fish, "set" that single, barbless hook, and don't give it slack until *you* are ready to shake *it* free.

Another method to see which way the water actually flows is simply to go to the top of a pool and throw a chip or a piece of beaver kill into the stream and watch where the water takes it. This will give you a fair idea where the stronger water is, what direction it takes, how fast, and consequently, the angle your cast should be. A beaver kill branch will float high, can easily be seen from shore, and will swing with the currents and indicate the little directions of the water's flow.

This knowledge will also tell you whether you should be fishing a slow- or fast-water fly, the angle of your swing, and the speed and length of cast you will need to reach the channel, which will be in faster water where there is more oxygen, especially in warm temperatures. While the holding areas become less obvious in freshet conditions and are harder to reach, your directed cast will remain the same, even if the water rises. I have also found that the lower the stream gets and the more bony it becomes, the more obvious the direction of its currents gets. At such times, there are places in a stream where the water is running at right angles to the main flow. Of course, these sub-flows are the same during higher water, only they are wider and less obvious. Their directions are chosen because of boulders on the river's bottom.

Old river wisdom about falling water says if the water is dropping very fast, it is a positive sign that before long it will rise again. Plus, the sour river smells of exposed eelgrass, algae, clam shells, and rocks are always stronger when the water is dropping. These are, according to old river folk, indications of an approaching rainstorm. My father used to say, "It's going to rain. I can smell the river from up here at the house."

On Reading the Water

But we should fish a pool as if the water were low, once these angles are discovered and the salmon lies are found. The smaller the pool, and indeed the stream, the more refined the presentation has to be. Everything should be considered because, in the little pools, a fish will move less and the fly hook has to be right on its nose before it is considered touchable. The speed of cast and how fast the fish want a fly in a given stretch of water are the whole story. Of course, when the river is up, fish will hold in places where there would not be enough water in low conditions, and everyone knows that a travelling fish will take the route of least resistance. At such times, it is important to not over-wade; rather, feel your way out to the heavy water.

If you have no idea where the fish lies are on a given stretch of water, you have to fish it all, inch by inch. Because sometimes a fish will lie in two feet of water, especially if it is bog-stained or teak-coloured. Start with a short cast, just the leader. Measure your casts, each one a fraction longer than the last, and move your feet gradually downstream. It's like mowing with a hand scythe in that each swathe must reach a fraction further, cover new ground, new water. This is time-consuming but effective. You still have to present your fly with the proper swing and speed, and this also becomes guesswork if you haven't read the water. Still, there are people who just love to cast a fly line, fish or no fish: reading the water is less important to them.

Some waters require a forty-five-degree angle cast. Others may demand a seventy-five- or even a ninety-degree swing. Most people fish the forty-five everywhere, don't retrieve, and give no thought to the water's speed. For example, the slower the water in a given stretch, the broader the angle of cast needed. It's almost that simple, but not quite. It's an educated guess because nothing is cut-and-dried in salmon angling: in the end everything depends upon the fish's state of mind. For fast or heavy water, the basic forty-five-degree angle taught in fly-casting schools is an easy rule of thumb for beginners. And today's fishers don't always have the luxury of angling in the strong, low water pools—certainly not in the valuable, cold-water holding areas. Our streams are becoming more crowded by the day as the fly-fishing fad grows and novice anglers head to our rivers in larger numbers.

When you think you have it all figured out, the river gods will turn against you, and you realize just how much about rivers and salmon you do not know. This holds true even if you've been on the water for three hundred years. But it is safe to say that in slow or dead water, the retrieve should be enhanced with a strip action to make sure the fly hits and moves instantly. Otherwise it will appear lifeless as it gradually sinks toward the bottom in the slow swing.

In slow-moving waters, river people fish the double-tapered lines instead of the weight-forward or torpedo tapers. The double taper has to be cast, not shot out, across the water. The well-cast line will have a higher and slower turnover and a bigger loop, which sets up the hand retrieve action before the fly hook even touches the water. It's a hit-and-move, hit-and-move action, and in short natural strokes like those of a water bug. (I call it the beaver stroke.) If you are raising fish that won't take your fly—especially if it is a deep, lazy roll—try broadening your angle and/or speeding up your retrieve. So often these fish want the fly to move a little faster because they strike on impulse.

A breeze can also tell you where the heavy water is in a pool, the so-called channel, especially if the wind is blowing upstream. In a breeze, there are always smooth areas on the water's surface that indicate where it is deep and also has the strongest flow. There are curving scrolls beside these smooth surfaces, and if the sun is bright, a scattering of crystals move in patch formations beside the point where the wind's power and the water's flow contrast. Where there is no flow (as in an eddy), the waves are more choppy and rolling. If it is a downriver wind, these surface patterns also hold true, although they are less obvious, unless of course the wind is stronger than the water's speed.

If we learn to observe these wind patterns, we can read the water's depth in any given place on a stream, even from well back on the shore, if there is any wind at all. We can also follow the river's main currents and their speeds simply by observing these wind patterns. In some ways, this is an abbreviated version of how someone might read the depth of an ocean or giant lake by the waves' height, the water's colours (as in the Caribbean Sea, where these colours change with the depth and texture of the ocean's bottom), or even the presence of seagulls, eagles, or osprey. By comparison, the channels where the Atlantic salmon are most likely to run are more obvious.

It is one challenge to find the true channel in a big river in even a moderate breeze, and quite another to get the fly hook out there in proper presentation. There are many great casters on the Miramichi. They had to learn how to be as children in order to reach these places and catch a fish for the dinner table. Like golfers playing the wind ball, there are always ways to make the wind work for you instead of against you.

For most, if you are on the left side of a stream facing downriver and are right-handed, an upriver wind will enhance your back cast. And if you cut your fore cast high into the breeze with lead space, the wind will carry out the line by keeping it in the air just a little longer. It is possible to cut a line without keeping it low, just as it is possible to cut a high golf ball. But instructors always recommend a low, tight loop into the breeze; just as hitting a low golf ball *into* the wind and a high ball *with* the wind is the safer play. As well, the tighter, lower cast into the wind becomes easier if you have heavier shooting tapers. Delayed wrist action, tight loops, and a late, low turnover combine for the desired swing in any pitch against the wind. However you get the fly out there, the cast angle and speed of the retrieve are the most important part of the presentation.

The Cains is a dark and slow-moving stream, and a cast has to be almost at right angles to be effective, or just short of horizontal, so there is no belly in the line and the fly moves across the water, not drifting downstream with the flow. One fall, when Georgia's Larry Kennedy and I were fishing Duffy's Run on the Cains River, we experimented with cast angles and retrieves. We observed a certain hand action was required to increase the fly speed. We held our casting lines against the rod grips with our index fingers and pulled it through in short jerks with the other hand. We found that by using a slow-water fly hook (say, the Ingalls Butterfly or the Green Machine), this stroke action made the wings and the long hackles swim across the surface like an insect. Locally, this retrieve is called the "Cains River Stroke." But my friend Larry, who was an Orvis dealer and a tarpon guide on St. Simons Island, referred to it as the "Strip Tease," a stroke he had used for that saltwater game fish. This was not only a more sexy title, but a more accurate one, as these fish were aggressive and quickly approaching the spawning grounds.

Personally, I grew up fishing slow or dead water and, in that sense, had learned the most effective way to "strip" at an early age.

There's a place in Black Rapids where I used to go with a client I was guiding. If I tossed a chip into the water at the top of the run, it drifted on an angle that took it almost to the opposite shore before it got to the "bottom" or downriver end of the pool. This meant that my guest had to cast at right angles from the direction in which the river appeared to be flowing from the shore. Many fish were hooked and lost because the fly was presented at the wrong angle, hence the wrong speed. And everyone knows that a fish will not hook well on a straight up-and-down cast. I have seen this done by fishers who have been on the river for many years: they just did not take the time to look closely. When I told them the angle required, they wouldn't believe me. Of course, someone who has been fishing for decades does not want a lecture on speed and angles, not from me. So I had to learn to say nothing and let these fishers do it their own way.

When I was guiding, I made it my practice to tell my clients the proper angle and speed required on a given stretch of water, first thing. Beginners would follow my advice. Well-seasoned anglers, who have been in the habit of casting a forty-five-degree line for many years, would follow my advice only for a while and then would slip back into old habits, like an incorrectly grooved golf swing a player has been living with for decades. So I left it to those clients to fish at their own leisure and with their own bag of tricks. And if they wanted to meditate, it was all the same to me—all in a day's work.

Fly-Tiers I Knew

When I was a schoolboy, I looked upon fly-tiers as demigods, people who could take a duck or a hen feather, a grey or a red squirrel's tail, and turn it into a feathered or hair-wing classic. This was nothing short of artwork. And the characters who did this were creative and artistic: they made things happen on the river and elsewhere. Without them, my life would have been dull and boring.

When I started salmon angling in the early fifties, I got my fly-hooks at a small fly-tying shop in Blackville. Everett Price (an upriver name) had a small shack beside his home where he tied flies for the river outfitters and the big outdoor suppliers. At that time, Mr. Price was an asthmatic old man who played violin by note, read good literature, but otherwise kept busy at his fly-tier's bench. I traded feathers, squirrel tails, and deer tails for the classic hooks that he became famous for, having supplied the big world outfitters for a lifetime. He took the tails and feathers I brought to him and transformed them into the most beautiful fly hooks imaginable: classic patterns like the Grey Ghost, Silver Grey, Silver Doctor, and of course the Oriole, a fly hook that has a mallard wing, black hackle, and a golden pheasant tail, and which became the luckiest fly pattern of my early years. I landed hundreds of grilse and salmon on that hook. Years later, after my mentor had passed on and I had built my own cabin on the river, I named the place Camp Oriole after that productive boyhood fly hook. And even today, when I see an

Oriole fly hook or hear the strains of a violin, I think of Everett Price and my early days of angling my old home stream.

Everett Price always had time for me as a youngster. I was fascinated with what his big hands could do, both with the violin and at the fly-tying vice. My two passions as a child were fiddle music and fly-fishing. I played the Price violin and I fished Price salmon flies. I got my first salmon when I was eight years old while angling with the Price fly hook. I had been playing Mr. Price's violin at house parties and dances along the Miramichi even before that. Of course, I had an instrument of my own in those early years: a ten-dollar fiddle I had bought from Eaton's mail-order catalogue. But Mr. Price's violin was more expensive and had better sound. So he let me use it when I performed, without a sound system, in front of noisy crowds.

Artistic to his fingertips, yet meticulous, Mr. Price always lectured me on how to look after his violin, how to keep its varnished top free from a build-up of rosin dust—a sound-muting occurrence commonly ignored among country violin players—and my greasy hands away from the bow's sensitive, gum-rosined hair, which he said had been strung from the tail of a white horse.

When Everett gave me a fly hook fresh off the vice, he would say, "Now don't you touch this until you fish it."

He said the feathered wings on any hook would stay in the appropriate position after an evening's angling, and could not be tufted out of place thereafter, even if the fly hook was not properly looked after or kept in a case. It seemed like everything that came from Mr. Price was a lesson, whether it was about how to care for a salmon fly or how to hold the fiddle properly so that I could reach the different positions with all fingers. Indeed, the man was my boyhood mentor as well as my violin master. Preoccupied with these things around home, my father once told me I should learn to think outside the fly box and the "violin case." Even now, so many years later, when I see a classic Scotch pattern fly hook in a showcase or hear Mozart's Violin Concerto No. 1 in B-flat major, I think of Everett Price.

⌒

Emerson Underhill of Barnettville, New Brunswick, was another fly-tier from that old school of higher standards. At the time of his death in April 2017 he was considered one of the best in North America at his trade and had invented many fly-hook patterns, including the Green Machine and the Shady Lady, two of the most productive and sought-after fly patterns on this river. (It is said by the well-seasoned anglers that you need only two fly hooks to fish the Miramichi: a Green Machine and a back-up Green Machine in case you lose the original.) Emerson tied them in mass production.

For these accomplishments, as well as supplying so many retail stores with fly hooks through the years, Emerson Underhill was inducted into the Atlantic Salmon Museum Hall of Fame.

Paralyzed from the waist down, having suffered a near-fatal car accident in 1965 (a tragedy that now appears to have happened a hundred years ago), Emerson was in a wheelchair for decades. Besides his successful fly-tying business, he collected antique guns and violins. His walls were decorated with Winchester rifles as well as many age-old violins of significant folklore. (I believe the Price violin may have been there awhile back.) Sometimes I would go to Emerson's house for a bit of good conversation, a cup of tea, and he would laugh as he listened to me start up a squeak on one of those old fiddles.

His active violin was in its case under the bed. When I passed it to him, I observed that it was in tune, standard pitch. While Emerson described himself as a "diddly-dum" fiddler, when he picked up the instrument and started to play the "Ontario Swing," I could tell that he had been practising and was indeed a fine player. And I would make a false gesture as if I were attempting to get up and dance.

I had seen Emerson Underhill at the dances years before his accident and knew he had an interest in that kind of music. In those days, he was a truck driver and a trapper. But one day, as he laid the instrument aside and we sipped tea, we reminisced about the great players we had heard through the years and who we believed were the best in our neck of the woods, in the country even. We talked, too, of trucks and of wild game.

Often when I went there, Emerson was so used up that he had to lie in bed on his side and face the wall. And as we talked, I would look into a mirror to see his unquestionably sincere reflection. It saddened me to see my old friend in such despair. During one visit, he had just come home from the Miramichi Hospital where he had been treated for infection in his feet.

He said, "My feet pained even though I couldn't feel them. Fevered, I tossed and turned all night, thinking that I was in the wrong bed. And when I finally got to sleep, I dreamed that I was tying flies, all night, tying, tying, tying flies. So that when I woke up in the morning I was as tired as if I had done a good day's work. In the hospital the nurses fed me a bag of liquid antibiotics and I was back home here in a day or two."

I think he was the last of that old breed of fly-tiers I knew as a boy. He must have been a young man when I first went there for hooks in the fifties. Though by this time (in the way that things are equalized by the years' passing), we were of the same vintage.

⟜

Lou Butterfield, who used to spend his summers in Howard, New Brunswick, was likewise an excellent fly-tier. He was also a classical ballroom dancer. Butterfield had come from the United States to angle for salmon in the forties. He stayed at Allen's Fishing Camp, and for a time my uncle Eldon guided him. Lou fell in love with our river. He also fell in love with a woman from Howard, whom he married. He built a cabin on the riverbank, near the mouth of Black Brook, that great salmon pool he had purchased from George and Earl Porter. Near this, overlooking the pool, he constructed a fly-tying shack where he put together some of the finest fly-hook patterns I have ever fished. Mr. Butterfield angled a short part of every day, except when the water temperatures rose to above seventy degrees. Sometimes I fished there with my uncle Eldon who, having guided Butterfield—such a kind man—years before, had an open invitation to the pool.

I also played fiddle for Mr. Butterfield, who held dances in his cabin on Monday nights with free admission for everyone. Most of the community's adults went there to square dance, though some went to waltz and to jive. The teenage girls and boys hung around the entryway and watched all the excitement. I can still see Lou Butterfield, a tall man in khaki pants and tan shoes, scuffing around the dance floor. He swung the young women off their feet and stopped only long enough to wipe the sweat from his brow with a white cotton handkerchief before moving into another set. For fiddling, he paid me two dollars a night and all the water I could drink. Plus a few fly-hooks of the old Scotch pattern vintage.

One spring during the high water, before Mr. Butterfield had arrived from the United States, his fly-tying shop went adrift in the night. It sailed down around the bend in that big river and came ashore on the flats just below Charlie Campbell's horse pasture, which was just across from home. Upon his arrival weeks later, Mr Butterfield looked for his building all along that stretch of river but could never find it. Of course, he did not know the treed flood meadows and back bogans like the local lads did.

It was Harold Campbell who in mid-May discovered the twisted shack, which was well back from the river and by then hidden in a grove of new-leafed poplar. With pries and props, he straightened up the building and used it as his own tackle shop all that summer.

I can still see Harold coming out the door of that shed with some of the most bastardized and gaudy feathered patterns one could imagine. Sometimes he traded these to me for a pack of Sportsman cigarettes by the makers of Black Cat—which I had stolen from my father's store. We shared the tobacco and we used the fly hooks.

However, this stroke of good fortune was short-lived. The next spring, the water rose even higher than the one previous, and Butterfield's shed moved on down around the bend to God-knows-where.

⌒⟶

Harold Campbell, an inarticulate character and a crude fly-tier, had been brewed from the cauldrons of the river's exceedingly modest, if not impoverished, way of life. And he was not about to change. I can still see him walking, pigeon-toed, along that shore across from home: nodding forward, with his hands in his coat pockets, and wearing a baseball cap backwards on his brow with sprigs of unruly blond hair curling out from under the hat, a hand-rolled cigarette dangling across his chapped lips.

When he stooped to bail the boat, he would say, "But it ain't no use though, Wayne. There ain't no use in a lad beatin' 'imself ta death out there, when the fish ain't even up here yet."

Harold would say that, yes, but from the time the ice left the river in April until the season ended in the fall, he fished a part of it every day. It was as if, more than anything, he just wanted to be on the water. And this pull came, no doubt, from deprivation of more worldly things. It was a retreat more than an escape, as someone who does have more worldly experiences might look for a river to sail away on.

Harold fished the double-tapered lines as I did — and most local anglers on this stretch of river still do. During the fore cast, he would start retrieving line while his fly hook was still in the air so as to give it an instant hit-and-move effect. Harold had a retrieve action that kept the line coiling around his fingers, like someone spinning yarn. He fished tirelessly, but he always left the river long before dark as he was night blind. Later in the evenings, when he came to our place for a game of Auction Forty-Fives, he carried a big kerosene-fired horse lantern.

Sometimes Harold went to the dances up at Butterfields'. For this trek, he took with him a five-cell flashlight. I remember seeing him there, standing in the shadows, with the long chrome cylinder under his arm. He referred to Mr. Butterfield as "Ol' Diddley-Wit." Once during intermission, I went out and talked with him. With a silly grin on his face he told me that he had come to Howard to look for a woman, but found that everyone he approached was either married or already "knocked up!"

Recluse that he was, and somewhat lacking in social graces, Harold never found the woman of his dreams, although I knew he had a lover (at least in his mind) early on, before he had quit Keenan School in grade seven.

I also hunted with Harold. In the fall we looked for deer and partridge at the same time. In the frosty woods and river meadows, with his breath puffing clouds of steam, he walked ahead of me with the cut-over .303 Lee-Enfield. I followed behind with the old sawed-off .22 Remington. I now believe he wanted me along in the event that darkness overtook him.

Once when we were hunting and Harold was walking behind me for a change, he raised the big rifle quite near my right ear and fired it in the air. The sound was deafening, and the shock almost knocked me down. When I turned to him for an explanation, he was laughing.

"Now we're even," he said. "Last summer you hit me on the right ear with the boxing glove!" Yes, he had held a grudge all that time.

We had done these childish things together into manhood. But then one winter when Harold was approaching early middle-age, he was diagnosed with leukemia. He was put under the supervision of a Blackville doctor who, every so often, injected fresh blood into his veins. Of course, it was hopeless: as time passed, everyone could see that Harold's health was failing him.

Still, in the spring, animated by the season and the sparkling river in front of home, he stomped to the pool his last few times. While he was a mere shadow of his old self, and no longer strong, he had a new-found gratitude for life, and as a palliative patient appeared even more susceptible to the river's spirits. He basked in the evening sunshine with the refined pleasure of a wine-taster sampling an old vintage. It was as if those beautiful though forlorn sunsets, the downriver clouds in exaggerated flame—as in my father's paintings—reawakened some of his deepest and most melancholy thoughts. For he would give me a sad smile, as though he were recalling our shared times, and, yes, perhaps the fantasies of long ago, inner realities that would remain unspoken, like that first love in a white dress who one might grasp for in a dream but remains out of reach. Indeed, those reveries were all beyond reach by this time.

He did this for quite a few evenings, and for me it was like the old days when we went there to swap genealogies, fly hooks, cigarettes, and gossip, and to catch a fish to be shared at our respective supper tables. It was a time of reminiscence. Maybe he wanted to angle that old home water, which for him would have been the most peaceful place on earth, to the end without any regrets clouding his memory.

There are days, even now, when I'm angling here that I think of these fly-tiers, and always with positive feelings.

Fly-Tiers I Knew

I am not acquainted with the current-day fly-tiers of this river, although I know there are some good ones around here. Cathy Colford of Blackville, an excellent fly-tier, is employed by Curtis Miramichi Outfitters. (This shop on Main Street in Blackville is owned by Brock Curtis, who is a good fly-tier himself.) Cathy puts together the most refined and distinct fly patterns, both wet and dry, that I have ever fished. She is also a member of the Atlantic Salmon Museum Hall of Fame.

Bruce Waugh, also a hall-of-famer, works at W.W. Doak's tackle shop on Main Street in Doaktown. He is a master of his craft. This business is now operated by Jerry Doak, son of the late Wallace Doak, a world-class fly-tier whom I did not know but was a crony of my father's. Bruce ties the durable and easy-to-fish showcase and catalogue flies for the most famous and long-standing fishing supply store in eastern Canada, W.W. Doak and Sons. This business was founded in 1946 and is a great success story.

I know there are probably a hundred young closet and commercial fly-tiers on this river whom I do not even recognize. Perhaps their characteristics will be romanticized by the youths of their time, whose days on the river are more memorable because of their artistic talents.

I guess I am too much from the old school when it comes to river ethics and fly-hook patterns. The strategies I use carry with them the ghost of the men who taught me the game, both on the river and, indeed, at the dance hall. All have now become a part of my river's legacy.

The Deep and Dark Dungarvon
RIVER OF LEGENDS

I had parked near the Furlong Bridge in an area that had once been a government campsite, with barbecue pits and patches of bonfire ashes under tall spruce trees that surrounded a small clearing dappled with dandelion and blue violets. Through the branches, I could glimpse the chuckling river as I sat on the truck's tailgate and put on my wading boots and vest. Then, like old times, I baited my hook with a healthy glob of angleworms, leaving some wiggle room free at the end. Mosquitoes buzzed as I walked the converging paths to get above the bridge, where there was a small gravel beach. From there, the river took a sharp bend to the left—under a hemlock sweep—before it funnelled down against a rock-faced cliff and tumbled between pilings to flatten out under the spans, where it was shaded and deep, and the water's black surface was dappled with grasshopper spit of white froth.

Wading off that beach, I threw a few feet of line into the choppy water. My hook swung so fast it skipped on the surface. On my second cast—about fifteen feet, including the leader—with a lesser angle, a pan-sized speckled trout struck at the hook but let it pass. I made the same cast, but no other fish appeared. After a few more throws into the white water, I worked my way down toward what we call the Bridge Pool.

Ahead in the slower, darker water, I could see trout flipping on the surface. They were picking up some kind of hatch, I figured. Still, between you and me, for old time's sake I wanted to try the baited hook under those lambs of foam in that deep hole. I don't always come to this special place expecting to hook a fish, the bait hook being an old tradition I wanted to re-enact from boyhood. I have been fly-fishing this river and other Miramichi waters since before adolescence.

On this day — it was Victoria Day, May 18, 2015 — I came here for nostalgic reasons: for the atmosphere, for the memories, to relive the family's ancestry, and because this old river has a good soul and a wealth of legend that I have no desire to put away. In truth, the Dungarvon, black as pig iron and deep as a monastery, is the most intimate of all salmon rivers. She is modest and unassuming in her course, the rhythm of the water's steady flow, the cadence, the syntax, and the metre harmonized. If I could only learn to write that way, I think, to keep the narrative moving onward with such consistency and passion, such continuity. And always with the same consoling theme, the same positive message: "Welcome to my shore, old friends. I love you all."

Indeed, when this river of ink speaks to me, she offers a kind of prose that words cannot convey. It is more a feeling to be given over to meditation, perhaps even prayer. We are left to think and take from the river what she has to offer, as she connects us, from man to man, woman to woman — the mindset of the ones who have meditated here before us — with the understanding that only a river can provide as a healer to the soul. I have said to her many times, "You are my soul's keeper; you are my passion and my parish." Yes, it is better than books, better than rehab, better than church. It is like a new kind of self-creation brought forth by the wilderness and the stream. I have felt this connection. I have seen it in others. It goes deeper than romance and is much more reliable.

Indeed, she is always here for me.

Until the big rains come. Then the river triples in size, becomes angry and threatening, careless, and no one dares to cross her or relate to her mood as she takes on a new hurried course, exceeding her banks while galloping down the channels, like frightened cattle stampeding under the low-hanging hemlock branches.

The ice floes are another matter, as were the log jams of my grandfather's day. At times like those the river took on a new meaning, one of recklessness, openness, show, and the prospect of commerce.

Fly-fishing was then, and still is, a religion in our family. The Dungarvon has never been academic, confined to the facts, or taken for granted. And that is where her beauty lies. I feel this, even when I am driving on the gravel road—past the ice cream stand, the church-yards, the huckleberry school grounds, the abandoned farms—from the village of Blackville.

The soul of my grandfather, a river man and a log driver, remains in Dungarvon—especially at this time of year—as does the spirit of his first cousin "Rovin'" Joe Smith, who wrote the much-anthologized folk song "A Winter on Renous." The haunting and tortured soul of the Dungarvon Whooper is strong up near the Whooper Spring, along with all the men and women who have come here to fish and have felt its spooky presence. The spirit of my late ex-wife, Janet, is here, along with those of my sons, Jeff, Jason, and Steven, back when they were children. And our old Irish setter, Shane, is splashing and then swimming against the water's flow. If I listen carefully, I can hear their voices in the water's chuckle, the pine trees' sighing. Happy are those who live in history, I think. They are all gone now, tired of the old ways, having moved on to more exciting things, bigger places, for sure higher up in the new world order.

But for me, those people are here and will not go away. It is an internal sense of company, like anything we might become intimate with. Just as you cannot judge a play from the audible applause, you cannot judge a river by a canoe trip gone sour. "Dogs bark but the caravans move on."

$\smile$

The Dungarvon, small and fast flowing, sweeps through the rolling hills of eastern New Brunswick and finds its way into the Miramichi via the Renous. This river, though quite consistent in salmon catches for its size, is primarily an early-run salmon stream, and if it were anywhere else in North America, it would get a lot more attention. Like most rivers that are easy to reach, it would be overfished. Being overshadowed by the main river, the big Southwest Miramichi, this productive little stream is often overlooked by anglers; indeed, this tributary is probably the best little salmon stream in a province known for its great Atlantic salmon watershed.

I can recall when my boys were small in the mid-seventies, their mother, Janet, and I brought them to this spot on this same holiday weekend. We had a picnic on the gravel beach and roasted marshmallows. I threw dry flies into the choppy area and hooked a bright salmon that was as big as a snowshoe. That day, the salmon boiled deep and there was not much wake behind the hook, in the way that a big trout might do, and I thought that was what I had on the line. But when I set the hook, the salmon took off in a long run, down under the bridge and jumped right out of the water. Wow! And I knew I had my hands full with that lightweight tackle. I struggled to accommodate the big fish, which stayed on my line for a good ten minutes before the number 12 trout hook popped out on a head shake. I spent the rest of the afternoon cursing those fingerling speckled trout. I fished until the tree's shadows on our side reached across the river, and then up the hillside, and we knew it was eight o'clock, time to drive back to the village and on to Keenan, where our cabin stands.

Sometimes Janet took her turn with the rod while I hung out on the beach with the children, playing catch with a tennis ball.

In my grandfather's day there were bright salmon in the Dungarvon as early as late April. He told me that he had hooked a bright fish further upstream while log-driving. This was in an area that we now refer to as the Red Pine Landings, a stretch of choppy water where from up on the highest point of the landing site, at the old prison grounds that serve as a parking lot, you can see around three bends in this turbulent little river. Papa said that it was in the first bend — at the foot of the log jam — that he hooked a bright salmon on a hook he had baited with a pork rind. The log drivers had camped there for the night, and some of the men took to fishing, but no other salmon was hooked. Papa cleaned and buried his shiny fish in the coolness of a nearby snowbank, only to have it eaten in the dark of night by hungry bears. My grandfather, always superstitious, felt at first that it may have been stolen by the ghost of the Whooper. Of course, the bear tracks were the giveaway.

The Whooper Spring, which is just around the bend and not far into the woods, has the most famous ghost in eastern Canada: the Dungarvon Whooper. According to legend, a lumber camp tragedy occurred in the early twentieth century, when the camp cook was robbed and murdered, and his remains had to be buried in the woods because the snow was too deep to bring the body out to the community for proper interment. Great whoops came from that gravesite, causing days and nights of unrest for the woods crew, until

Father Murdock, the Roman Catholic priest from Saint Bridget's in Renous, was brought in to exorcise the gravesite, and the screeching stopped.

There was a poem and a song written about this incident by Michael Whelan, the famous poet from Renous (1858–1937). Each stanza ends with the words, "Where the deep and dark Dungarvon sweeps along." There has also been a popular stage play written by local playwright Bernie Colepaugh that is performed annually by the Miramichi Heritage Players, a theatre group in Renous. In Blackville's municipal park, there is a chainsaw-carved statue of the Whooper in his full "whooping" mode. So the spirit, the legend, is strong here.

For years I had listened to my grandfather tell fireside stories about the Dungarvon River. He talked of the famous Salmon Hole where he and his cousin Joe Smith, working out of a dugout canoe, speared a truck-wagon load of fall salmon to supply a lumber camp with fish for the winter. It had been on a wet day when they had nothing better to do. They may have taken back a bull moose as well, had they brought a gun.

"We saw three bulls in the river," Papa said.

And Papa told log-chopping, log-driving stories, caribou-hunting, and bear-trapping tales to stir a youngster's imagination.

Joe Smith, who had been a trapper, drowned in Holmes Lake in the early winter of 1912, when he dropped through the ice on his way out of the woods for the Christmas holiday. It was said that he broke ice for a long way — losing his fingernails in the process — before finally succumbing to the icy waters. His body was recovered the next day in nine feet of water, nine feet from shore. Joe was laid to rest in Saint Bridget's old cemetery in Renous. I have been there to lay a twig on his headstone.

The Deep and Dark Dungarvon

When I first came home from Ontario in the spring of '69, I could not get enough woods and river, especially the Dungarvon. I had traded my old convertible for a good second-hand white station wagon with a 409 engine, tinted windows, air conditioning, and a good tape machine. That vehicle served my family not only as a means of transportation but also as a camp. Janet and I fished out of the car and took turns backpacking one-year-old Jeff, our first son. I had purchased a few canvas deck chairs and a felt mattress, which we put in the back of the car after the rear seat was folded down. This became our bedroom. Using a portable charcoal barbecue, we cooked on the windy tailgate and used the car's hood for a table. We bathed in the river and drank brook water. I can still hear the songs of the day blasting from the rear speakers: Bob Dylan's "Mr. Tambourine Man" and Joni Mitchell's "Urge for Going" and "River."

Later in the summer, we stayed for a week on the Dungarvon in an abandoned log-drivers' scow that had come adrift and lodged in the trees on a flat not far from the high-water mark at the Salmon Hole. Even though the shack was unsightly and unclean, it was equipped for cooking, had sleeping quarters, and made a good shelter from the flies and rain. We gave it a quick clean-up and it became our secret camp, until one evening when I was having a few drinks and cooking a late meal, the tarpaper behind the stove caught fire. Try as we did with buckets and brooms, we could not save the scow. It burnt to the ground and might have taken a stand of trees had there been a wind.

Now, as I wade downstream toward the bridge, again I can see trout rolling and splashing at insects on the surface. At the bridge, I make a few casts, a few swings, a few dangles, but nothing. Then I notice insects buzzing about and lighting on the side of the cedar abutment, some kind of mayfly hatch I suspect. I pick up one of the long-legged grey-winged flies that my son later told me would have been a Green Drake. Having fished salmon all of my life, I know nothing about matching the hatches. But this one was obvious. From my fly case, I tie on my leader the nearest thing I had — a number 6 Oriole — and make the cast. The wings' beat of the fly hook, shadow upon shadow, swing partially submerged under the bridge, and suddenly I am getting strikes. Yes, I release all my trout back into the stream, though some I believe are trophy size. To me it is more important to have the fish here for the fishing. It was a part of the lure that helped to keep the great spirit of the river alive, so why destroy that?

Those early-run salmon are invisible, though always present. They are ghosts themselves. While I have hooked and landed many big salmon on this stream, I now come to the Dungarvon not for the fish but rather for the atmosphere, the memories. It is still a great place to relax, throw a line, be at one with those deep and dark waters, relive a bit of family folklore in a place so steeped in legend. When I am here, I can see my grandfather and his contemporaries in their high hobnail boots, unravelling the log jams with their spears and picks. I see my father and his brother-in-law, Ralph Warren, on those legendary deer hunts of the fifties. And also, in the sounds of the water and the birdsong, there are echoes of my young family, alive and well, as we eat lunch on that gravel shore above the Furlong Bridge.

And I think, this is a river that gives back in many ways.

Fishing the North Pole

The North Pole is a turbulent stream that flows into the Little Southwest Miramichi, just upriver from the confluence of Catamaran Brook, which is high in New Brunswick's interior. The place is famous for its many fast-water holding pools, big salmon and trout, spectacular scenery, and an imposing spirit.

This stretch of river is still owned by the provincial government and is known locally as Crown Reserve Waters. To get a chance to fish there, you have to apply through the Department of Natural Resources in Miramichi and get lucky in a draw that takes place in the early spring. This raffle is for New Brunswick residents only and has long since been shortened to two-day excursions, with a last-minute online application program for parties of four for a one-day trip in the event of cancellations. Of course, all angling in this region has long since been designated hook-and-release waters and with barbless hooks.

In the summer of '72, my father, my brother Herbie, a friend Johnny Carnahan, and I travelled to this stream for a three-day fishing expedition. The dates we were given in our draw were July 12 through 14. On July 11, we left Millerton for the North Pole Stream, travelling almost forty miles in two vehicles. The roads were terrible up in those heavily wooded hills — the forest was stunted black and red spruce with a scattered series of mosquito-infested bog holes — and even though my station wagon was quite high, as we got nearer to our destination, the boulders were closer together and bigger so that my oil pan and muffler were scraping them.

I decided to park my vehicle a few miles from the river, at a fish warden's camp, and we loaded our provisions into the back of Johnny's bigger, four-wheel-drive half-ton. Herbie and I climbed on the back of the truck and sat on the luggage in the rain as Johnny's vehicle crawled over what was indeed miserable terrain. There were bear-shaped and trunk-shaped boulders and long shallows of muddy water where our driver shifted gears as the truck laboured through, spinning brown water against the roadside shrubs and up into the limbs of the spruce.

The altitude was high and with the rain coming down it was cold, even in mid-July. As the truck laboured along and we were tossed from side to side, Herbie reached into a piece of luggage and brought out a pint of Scotch whisky, opened it, and we each took a long swig that tingled our insides and warmed us up slightly. We smoked cigarettes as we braced ourselves and hung onto the truck's box to keep from falling over the side.

When the road ended in a small clearing, Johnny parked the truck. We unloaded the provisions that we had to portage on our backs for the last few hundred yards to a brown camp called Ramsey Lodge, a quaint log cabin with a veranda facing the wildest of all rivers. Long before we got near the river, we could hear the roar of the water, the grinding of rocks under the rushing torrents. These river sounds would become more amplified in the dark of night as we tried to sleep in the stale-smelling camp. Though tolerable, with a cook-range, an oilcloth-covered table, kitchen chairs, and four straw bunks, it was a camp whose greatest value was measured by its proximity to the North Pole Stream, which was tumbling past just a stone's throw from the front veranda. (That old cabin has since been torn down and replaced by a new, more modern structure.) At that time, these waters were filled with a sense of mystery, as all new and unfished rivers are. In truth, it was a stream that aroused more curiosity than admiration. But considering the laws of probability, we expected to catch fish.

Indeed, Ramsey Lodge sat on the shores of one of the rockiest and most turbulent little rivers any of us had seen. The black water in that swamp-fed lower stretch, having risen following the rains, was spilling into a frothy torrent as it descended over a series of ledges that were shaped like a long, spiral flight of stairs. Just upstream from the cabin, there was a pool called Palisade. This was a good-sized waterfall, gushing between two sharp ledges of black granite and twisting at the foot into a deep whirlpool where we knew salmon were holding. Having walked to the foot of the falls, we could see the fish jumping against the full volume of the water, holding in the currents as they tried to make it over to more friendly waters. Sometimes it took two or three attempts to gain the challenge of the Palisade, move on to the upper stretch, which was another parcel of pools the government was raffling.

Other pools along the stretch were Jack Pots (One and Two), Table Rock, Camp Pool, and less than a half mile downriver, Anthony's Hole, which is a big beaver dam–like dead water where salmon played like shad in the evenings. This was where, in the old days, a log driver's body, Anthony, had been found after he had drowned upstream at the Palisade Falls. It is said that he had been trying to free a log jam, and the rope he was lowered down on with the dynamite broke. He fell into the rapids and was sucked under the jam. Anthony's hobnail driving boots had been nailed to a spruce tree, an epitaph at the edge of the water, and after fifty years, they were still hanging there, decayed but intact. The old log-landing sites on the forested hillsides along the Pole were still visible.

We got dressed to go fishing. Johnny, suffering with arthritis, did not go out that evening because his joints were aching from the dampness. He sat, slouched down in a canvas chair on the veranda, a cigarette in hand, as was his habit. The rest of us hiked through waist-high bracken to the Camp Pool, which was a short stretch of frothy water where the river hurried around a ledge. On the shore, at the top of Anthony's Hole, there was an abandoned log cabin built by the Pratt family many years before when they had leased this stretch from the government for the outfitting trade. We took turns fly casting this little stretch, and I believe we hooked something like eight salmon on that first evening. The water was fast and cold, and the fish were jumping and rolling as they moved upstream on the rise. They rose for any fly pattern we threw over them. The trees standing so close to the water made casting a problem, and sometimes we had to roll-cast to get our lines out to the fish. I can remember standing on a fallen tree and watching my brother cast a fly hook over three salmon resting in Anthony's Hole. All three fish chased after his fly at once.

We found the fish up in this high country were skinny compared to the main river salmon. We supposed their weight loss was from having climbed so many rapids to get here. So we did not kill a fish even though, back then, we could have brought out two fish a day each. It seemed a shame to take a salmon that had gone through so much rugged terrain to get here.

There were converging paths among the waist-high sally bushes — the muted hum of bees in the summer's bloom — fringing this small, bony river that sparkled like diamonds among the stunted black and red spruces. And on the riverbed there were rocks the size of cars, even minivans, and others were more like tractor-trailers to climb over to get to the salmon. As I hiked along the river I can remember thinking that these fish are like an old love in that happiness lay not in possessing them but rather in the search for them.

Later in the camp, as Johnny cooked the evening meal, someone lit the Coleman oil lamp and a thousand bluebottle flies came from out of the woodwork to fill the camp. Buzzing at the glass, they made a dark cloud around the lamp's glow. We had to open the door and use brooms to fan them outside. It seemed to be too cold for mosquitoes, even though we could feel a cow's breath of south wind that whispered through the screen door and that my father said meant that we would have a few fine days ahead. And there was the gravedigger's inhalation of tobacco smoke, the scent of Scotch whisky. The cabin was clean otherwise, and the big wood stove that had no back or warming closet—which, according to local fish warden Jim MacDonald, had been lifted in here by helicopter years before when Mr. Pratt built the place—was adequate for Johnny to cook all kinds of vegetables and to fry pork chops. And to brew the ten-minute-boiled river water for tea. MacDonald had been a friend of my brother's and was staying at the green ranger camp a few miles out, where I had left my station wagon. He was in the government's employ for the summer. Each evening Jim dropped in to check on us, and he always stayed for a drink and for supper, joining the party around the big camp table. (Jimmy MacDonald has since passed on and is now a warden in the sky.)

Outside, the sky had cleared and the beautiful post-sunset had turned the frothing river into a flow of noisy red lava. And then the cold night moon peeked over those stunted treetops to bring its own watery reflections of dancing brass. Sometime in the night, we heard grunting and banging outside when a bear—or was it a raccoon—got into our predecessor's garbage and upset the plank storage bin. This brought us out of our bunks, half asleep, to huddle on the veranda with flashlights as we tried to glimpse the animal that had by then disappeared into the undergrowth. Across from the cabin at the dancing water's edge, a grassy sod hung over a tangle of roots, wrinkled like the pop-eyed face of an elderly fisherman. For sure, that old river was full of night magic.

On the second day, it was sunny and warm. After a breakfast of fried ham and eggs, we hiked along the river, following those crooked paths through the purple sage, and climbed ledges to get into position to test the many pools that appeared to be almost unfishable. There were places where we had to hold our tackle over our heads to keep it from tangling in the shoulder-high underbrush. The water was moving so fast that it was hard to get our fly hooks to make a decent swing over the fish. But the salmon were still chasing after our hooks. We had never seen fish come to flies so easily, and we soon became bored with it.

Herbie and I had brought our old guitars on the trip; we played music and sang in the folk era. Through the heat of the day, as Father and Johnny fished or slept, we hiked in separate directions along the choppy river's course. We had the intention of stopping at some stretch of fast water and, getting our inspiration from the freshet sounds, writing a piece of music. Through the afternoon we sat beside different pools at different ends of the stretch and tried to put the water lyrics into proper pitches, to capture the spirit of the place, a B-flat sentimental spill, an A-minor melancholy riffle, a C-sharp romantic rapid, and so on.

Later that day, when we returned to the cabin to compare our notes and play our tunes for one another, we found that we had separately written very similar pieces. These tunes I carried in my head for a long time afterward, and they always took me back to that place on the North Pole Stream, although they have long since been forgotten because we did not write them down. Strangely, after being apart for most of the day, when my brother and I got together, we were humming a Beatles song, "And I Love Her." It seemed to come to both of us from out of the water and its surroundings. It's funny what comes out of landscapes and riverscapes sometimes, how it is translated into an art form. For sure, that stream was a great place to meditate, and

I was vitalized and inspired by its spirit in the same way that water in a vase nourishes a wildflower. I wanted to write about it. I wanted to do a film.

Late in the afternoon, I made tea on the shore at Camp Pool and served it to Father and Johnny, who had fished the morning and were having the time of their lives, even though the fishing had tightened up somewhat from the evening before as the water began to drop and warm up. They had taken only two grilse while we were away.

That little fishing trip to the North Pole Stream was one of the best river experiences that I can remember from the early seventies, though we brought home no fish. The scenery was wonderful, our adventure tinged with legend: the steep log-landing sites, the rustic log cabins, Anthony's spooky old driving boots visible at the water's edge. Most of all, the company — Johnny, my father, and Herbie — seemed to blend together to make a spirited party whole. As though we had been casted, we all seemed to be the right age for the parts we played. The presence of the older men seemed a nice contrast to our carefree party attitudes, the romances Herb and I were experiencing. In my case, it was a protest against society, left over from the sixties when I had lived in southern Ontario.

To me, for better or worse, nostalgia aside, the spirit of youth is a thing that neither money nor romance can recapture down the road. As we age, we lose our vigour and free-spiritedness with the more refined vintage. My ex-brother-in-law Bob Miller — now a United Church minister in Fredericton — and I have had this argument many times. It is too bad that the mature mindset cannot take hold early on while still experiencing youth's heartiness.

At that early age we were fools, though we did not realize it. For why else would we travel over such rugged terrain, fight flies and foul weather, sleep on straw bunks in a stinking camp in order to chase after a fish? Mature adults do not do such things.

"It was the youthful spirit of living," I tell Bob, "a passionate zest that became lost in maturity and was hopefully replaced by wisdom."

⁓

Because reflections from that trip years before had stayed with me, during the early eighties when my sons, Jeff, Jason, and Steven, were small, I took them to the North Pole Stream for a day's fishing each August. At the house in Millerton, we packed a big lunch, plenty of drinks, and our fishing equipment into my new station wagon and took that early-morning drive over those long gravel hills and down through the deep valleys. The blue shadows of the trees reached over the car; the chrome sparkled when the sun hit us. My sons loved that drive and the superb stretch of water just as I did. For a time it became a kind of pilgrimage for us, a sacred place to go to be together and share a genuine wilderness spirit. We took photographs of each other standing beside some waterfall or camp skeleton. We always lunched in the Ramsey Lodge and fished the same waters with the same flies. The spirit of those adventures was still there when the family began to scatter and the boys went off to college.

By that time, it was no longer about the fishing; rather, it was for the atmosphere that we returned to the Pole, an ambience of log drivers, legends, and ghosts, the wilderness experience, something we all liked, and which I suppose we were trying to hold on to. At the lower end of Anthony's Hole, we always waded across the river to take a look at the boots that were by then unravelling at the soles. While we no longer had the same enthusiasm about catching fish, we had great salmon angling in water that was so cold and pure we could drink it.

My brother and his friends went there too, repeated times, not so much for the fish but for the ambience. And they wrote music. They were more into writing songs than I was, and had a band by then.

⌒

Long after my father was able to fish, he liked to talk about it when we got together, and we often reminisced about that special river experience on the North Pole Stream. He was no longer agile enough to venture that far afield, unless it was in a dream or a memory. When I went to the North Pole afterwards with my sons, I would think of my father in his younger days and also my dear friend Johnny, who died shortly after that first trip. His arthritis had all but crippled him physically when cancer came along to take his spirit away.

There was a point when none of us had gone to the North Pole for a long time. It just seemed impossible to get that many people together to stay anywhere for any length of time. Still, in the late eighties my sons, my brother-in-law, Phil Cassidy (who had also taken up fly-fishing by then), and I took a drive up that long dusty road for a two-day trip. We had gotten the necessary government permission in the City of Miramichi. Approaching the Pole, I drove my new car over that big hill toward the river on that still very rocky road. And again, the bottom scraped on the boulders. This time there was a summer student employed to monitor our catches. It was August, and the wild cherries were just turning red, a good three weeks behind those berries along the main river. Later, as we were preparing to go fishing, we detected the odour of gasoline. When we checked under the car, we found a punctured hole in the gas tank and the liquid was dropping fast onto the ground.

Phil went into the nearby Ramsey Lodge and found a vinegar jug and a piece of tarpaper. He fashioned a funnel, to put into the top of the jug, and we sat it under the drip. We were able to catch the gas and recycle it back into the tank. One of us took turns tending to this, while the others hiked and fished. It was that kind of place.

We went to the North Pole Stream every summer until there was no North Pole Stream, not the one of our memories. Through repetition and commonness, the subject matter could not compete with the art or the romance, our perception of how it used to be. So much of what we had been doing was in our minds.

Now that I am old and looking for God, the memories of those early expeditions bring me to a youthful state of mind that is somewhere between perfection and divinity.

"Yes, I have to look back to get fulfilment," I tell Bob Miller. I know I will go there someday with my sons for a day's fishing. I guess the road has been improved, so that I can go all the way over the hill to recapture those old fishing waters.

Fishing the Black

In early June of '94, George Curtis and I loaded benches into the plywood motorboat and with the little seven-horsepower Johnson Seahorse, distributed them to the different pools. While I had been guiding on the Miramichi River off and on for decades, this was my first experience at George's salmon camp, the Black Rapids Lodge. I would work for the next fourteen years on this part of the home stream, a coveted two-mile stretch of turbulent water, some of which had been acquired from Boston Red Sox player Ted Williams. Located between the Gray and the White Rapids, this property included the old Dower and the Porter Rapids, that is, the "Home Pool." Some of this water was under a private lease, but most was owned by the lodge—or, like the Harris Bar, it was government-owned or what is known in these circles as "open water." But all the holding pools were inaccessible to the public and protected by the great ledges and the absence of a legal right-of-way. (The old Harris place is where my great-grandmother Elizabeth Harris was born and lived until she married my great-grandfather David Curtis in the mid-1800s. The Harris Bar was in front of her house.)

All of the Black Rapid pools were fishable at different times of the season and at diverse times of the day, and indeed at different heights of water. It was the prettiest and most rugged stretch of river and landscape that I had seen to that point, and I had been fishing the Miramichi River, among others, since boyhood.

But on this day with George, there were times when the motor would not push the overloaded boat against the currents (especially in the turbulent Home Pool), and we had to leave a bench on the shore with plans to return for it later.

These were the plank love seats where George and I would sit at poolside with our guests and watch for a fish to move. We fought the heat and the mosquitoes in high summer—the water felt warm in the mornings, when the air was still cool—and drank brandy-sweetened tea by a fire on cold autumn days of rain and wind, and smoked mini-cigars, as was the custom for anglers at that time. We flattered our guests with moments of triumph, real or imagined.

Drifting downstream from Black Rapids, the pools were called Bathtub, Stan's Run, Ray's Rock, Delbert's Rock, The Reef, Buzz's Bar, Annie's Rock, Lyle's Run, Grilse Alley, Home Pool, Harris Bar, Oak Tree, and Line Pool. Many of these salmon holding areas were named after guests who had frequented the lodge and had had success there. Others, like the big Rock of Gibraltar–shaped stone at the top of the reef, were named after river guides like Delbert Coughland, who spent his work time sitting on the rock and smoking cigarettes while shouting directions to his clients. Sadly, at the age of fifty, Delbert died from a heart attack on a winter's morning in 2003.

In my decade and a half of guiding at Black Rapids, there was never a time I took a guest to any of those pools that we did not see fish of some kind. The water was black as mountain coffee and there was a dreamy foam line that trailed down the geometric centre of the stream. From the cabins—they sit on a bluff overlooking the water—the river reminded me of stretches of the Niagara, where it winds its way through the great gorge below the falls, and in places is just as frothy and exciting. At other places, it was dark and sullen and reminded me of Joseph Conrad's Congo.

Fishing the Black

There were right ways to fish these pools if you wanted to hook and land a salmon. Of course, George and I knew the angles and the speed of retrieve that each one required. I had learned from George, who grew up on this stretch of water. And we knew the times of day and water temperatures—when the air and water synchronize—when certain angles and speeds of cast worked best. The angles were anywhere from thirty degrees (with a free-swinging drift) in the frothing Home Pool, to ninety degrees in the still-water Line Pool, where we used a hit-and-move "strip tease" or "beaver stroke" action like we did on the Cains, a slow-moving tributary also of dark origins. The best times were between eleven in the morning at Buzz's Bar to seven in the evening, the old witching hour, at Line Pool. And there were a hundred angles and times in between.

For example, 6:30 p.m. at the Bathtub Pool in low water conditions was dynamite, whereas 10:20 a.m. in high water favoured Ray's Rock. River conditions considered, these were the most productive times and angles. Both guides and guests knew them and tried to be at the given pools at the right moments. (The guests fished the pools in rotation.) Although on a river anything can happen, and will happen, to make a liar out of the guide.

Once, a cow moose being chased by dogs fell over the high ledge in back of the Bathtub Pool. The animal had broken its neck and was lying dead in the pool, its stomach swollen, and with a dozen carrion birds feasting on the entrails. The scene looked like something you might have come across on the Amazon. The carcass made an unbearable stench that could be detected on the other side of the river, or if the wind was up, as far downstream as the Home Pool. The remains stayed there for two weeks—until the river rose—and in the night, it drifted down past the camp, its smell overtaking that of the river blossom and the water. Later in the summer, at Line Pool, we found its leg bones, bleached white, having been picked clean by the birds. Barring such rare calamity, the best overall consistency and the best catch averages per hours fished were at these times and places.

This paradise, the old Curtis property for many years, had the title Black Rapids Salmon Club, and there was a small American membership initiated by Maine's Foster Gordon, with George as manager. However, according to George, most of the members had sold back to him or had died by the time I arrived there to work. So it was George's operation and had long since taken on George's personality because it was indeed his old home water, hillside, trees, and cabins. There was a swampy place on the upper flats where, according to folklore, my great-grandmother Elizabeth Harris had lost a cow. And on the lower flat among cedar stood the Lack-a-Nookie Lodge, a saddleback pole cabin with a sunken veranda. The place had a ghostly lure, perhaps similar to that experienced by the characters in Conrad's *Heart of Darkness*. We used it as a guide's camp. This romantic icon of a cabin was purchased and later restored by Georgia's Larry Kennedy—a personal friend to George Curtis, Dennis Duffy, and me—because he loved its spirit.

For sure, there was great healing power at the Black, as we called it, some as a result of the scenery and some due to the down-home atmosphere nourished by the staff. And so it became a kind of home-away-from-home for the hundreds of fly fishers who came from far and near, sometimes two or three times during the long angling season. These anglers were treated to the best food and the cleanest camp quarters of any fishing lodge I had been to in the east. After a week's retreat here, everyone went back to Australia, Great Britain, the United States, or New Zealand happy, fish or no fish. And this rejuvenation we guaranteed.

Much of this healing effect could have been attributed to the gourmet cooking of George's wife, Jean, her sister Thelma, and George's sister Gloria. The housekeeping too was spic 'n span. I also believe that some of the operation's success could have been credited to the guides, who worked the long days wading into those frothy waters — there were slippery submerged boulders to step around — arm-in-arm with the guests, showing them the proper leader for a given water condition, the fly colour of the day, the length of cast, the line turnover required, while serving them streamside drinks they jokingly called Howard Road Tea and genuinely treating them as parents or grandparents.

I remember those guests as kin, once removed (without the DNA of a time-worn cousinhood), because a bond had developed between them, the guides, and the camp staff. Often they booked time at the lodge when the fishing was not great but because a certain guest, whose company they enjoyed, was also to be there. And this party would require special assignments for the camp staff and guides, arranging birthday parties and other celebrations. Yes, we took an interest in our clients, above and beyond what was the norm in the hospitality trade.

This bond worked two ways. I learned more about culture and the human condition from men like Frank Parker, a professor at Boston College who knew poet Robert Frost personally and had had him read to his class — Frost, wearing bedroom slippers, came down from New Hampshire on the bus the day before so he could see the Red Sox play — or Arthur Davenport, a contributor to the *New York Times*, than I did in any schoolhouse or university. These scholars and nature-lovers came here because the place had a distinct, romantic spirit, and the men and women fishers had personalities that blended into the scene to make the kinship with each other and the staff authentic.

When George and I get together now for a winter's evening of telephone chit-chat, we find ourselves going through a verbal list, recalling this one or that, the experiences shared with special people. Many of them are now long dead, for they were not young men and women when they fished the Black with us. These were people from the previous century living in that romantic *carpe diem* frame of mind, before anyone cared if a cigar and a glass of Scotch whisky were harmful to one's health. These people were more adventurous, better read, and better travelled when it came to rivers fished and fish caught than today's younger element.

Unlike with modern outdoor people today, there was no threat of liability held over the heads of outfitters and guides if anything went wrong. We were all risk-takers. I can remember an evening when a bolt of lightning snapped the fishing rod out of the hands of Tom Fuller, an outdoor writer and field editor from *Field & Stream* magazine. We had heard a rumble and were heading back to the clubhouse when lightning hit Tom's graphite. Luckily, he was not hurt.

I also recall a day when the canoe I was navigating went crosswise over the Porter Rapids with an old man seated in the bow. When I pulled the anchor, the motor refused to start. We hung on to the gunwales and drifted until the water slowed and I could paddle us to shore.

The next morning when I met my client in the dining room, he asked, "Are we going to fish today or whitewater raft?" It was a hard old joke for a seasoned river guide to swallow.

I have recollections of my guest Henry Walsh suffering hypothermia after standing for an afternoon in the sub-zero October river without long johns. At dark, when it was time to head back to camp, he was standing at the end of the moored canoe.

"I can't move my legs!" he said. "They are numb."

I had to lift him into the boat's belly and pole him back to camp, where George, Delbert, and I carried him up the hill to a warm cabin. Henry was vomiting by that time, and I thought he was having a heart attack. I called an ambulance that arrived with two paramedics. They examined Henry to confirm he would be okay. The next morning Henry was back out there in the water, again without the fleece-lined drawers.

Another time while fishing The Reef—a bar Ted Williams had bulldozed in centre stream years before—an upriver wind that came suddenly from out of nowhere blew my fisherman over into the rocky waters. To keep him from drifting away, I had to run and then wade to grasp him by an arm that was badly bruised, as was the side of his face. He was taken to Doctor Keenan in Blackville for first aid, but was back on the water later that day.

I saw an experienced young angler, a football player from New York State, go over his chest waders in Home Pool and almost drown before he got to shore. Every river person knows that when those long boots fill up with water, they will stand you on your head. Getting upright against the weight is as impossible as trying to lift and latch a sagging, weed-infested railway gate.

Once too, I capsized from having been passed too close by a high-speed motorboat with a probable drunk at the helm: the cross-chop upset the canoe with my guest and I in it. We had to hang on to the boat and swim to shore. The motorboat driver did not even look back to see if we made it to safety. Such is the quality, or lack thereof, in some river people.

There is an old saying among river guides that when you are on the water, everything that can go wrong will go wrong. This makes for good stories that become exaggerated with time and the brushstroke of nostalgia. I have a bag of them.

Back then, it was always the story that mattered, the adventure of getting out onto the water to relax and throw a line, bring back a tale. We didn't rely solely on storytelling, but it sure helped to keep guests contented in those dog-day stretches when the river was not producing, which is the way of all salmon rivers. It is funny how the simplest little river experience, retold under a certain influence at the dinner table, can become the main event of the day or even the summer.

I might have been an embedded journalist. I remember the fishers well. I can recall the time-enhanced experiences, too. I remember those conversations with people like businessman Doug Brown of Bangor, who gave me the advice to "never burn a bridge." Or with Casper Sergeant of Searsport, a Maine real estate man I loved like my own father. (I would trust him with my life's savings.) Or with Buzz Bezanson of Massachusetts (we had once planned to co-write a stage play). Uncle Ray Zukauskas from Midtown, New York City, wanted me to read landscape poetry to him while he fished. I operated his camcorder and gave him Frost and Wordsworth both in the water and on the bench. Uncle Ray died angling alone on a river in his home state, at a time of year when it was impossible for me to get to his funeral.

Having grown up in sight of this water, George could see a salmon move even before it left the river bottom. And this became a game he played with the guests, pointing to a wake or a boil and telling our guests that these were caused by the underwater actions of salmon.

"Yes, salmon; big salmon!"

Many of these wakes were not salmon, of course, and others would have been made by shad, gaspereau, sea-run trout, or even mudsuckers. Those big suckers would leap out of the water in mid and late summer and be mistaken for grilse. But they were all salmon in the eyes of us guides and consequently the eyes of our guests, who believed George, yet didn't believe George. For these people were salmon fishers only. This practice kept spirits up on the slow days between runs and made life a little more relaxing for guides who were trying to keep the fishers optimistic about their chances of catching a salmon. And it helped the guests to keep the confidence, one to another.

At that time, along the bends in that big river, there were treed summits on both sides, and these tall beauty strips — poplar, birch, cedar, and hemlock — were unbroken by landowners or would-be cottage builders. The shores along the high-water mark were decorated with tall lupines, violets, river lilies, and shore roses that smothered our walking trails through the grass, and around boulders from the clubhouse to the pools. These trails were later mowed with a scythe or bushwhacker. It was like a piece of river and landscape I had seen in England's Lake District, where William Wordsworth penned the great poem "I Wandered Lonely as a Cloud." The lupines were like a "coarse fish" version of the daffodil as they nodded and danced in the river breeze, outdoing the "waves in glee."

I used to tell my guests, "George has a paradise here."

Even now, two decades later, I dream of that shoreline with its stand of lupines and the sparkling purple water that chuckled amid the voices of songbirds. I can see every rock and blade of grass, every bird's nest. I can smell every cherry blossom. Yes, the forlorn scent of a cherry blossom along the sidewalk in town takes me back there. And I can feel every mood the great river laid upon us.

Sometimes in the evenings, George, wearing a white cotton apron, cooked steaks or boiled lobster on the big gas barbecue and served them to the guests. With wines and liqueurs, we laid a linen-covered table that stood under the pine trees in the lee of the wind. There was a lot of chatter and jostling for cigarettes and drinks amid the clinking of the ice cubes in the Scotch glasses, the jingle of silverware, the unfolding of the stiff linen napkins. It might have been a picnic lifted out of a Jane Austen novel.

After such a meal, the parties lasted into the late evenings, and from the toddies came singing and storytelling as spirits ran high. But river guides cannot stay and party with the guests after the fishing hours, not for long. They have to get back to the guides' camp for rest, as the long stretches on the river—sometimes weeks without a day off—in the wind, rain, or sunshine zaps energy. When it comes to dealing with people with frayed nerves who are themselves coming to camp for a bit of healing, it is a guide's responsibility to be there for them and be well, mentally and physically.

I recall one autumn when I was on the river for fifty-five days in a row. During lunch time each midday, I drove ten miles to my own cabin—Camp Oriole—on the Howard Road, put together a lunch, carried in the night's firewood, and took a short nap before heading back to Black Rapids Lodge for the evening fishing. One day a week, I took the midday break to drive to Miramichi (twenty miles each way) to do my laundry in a laundromat. I ate in a restaurant and did my banking while the clothes were drying. By the end of this stretch, of course, I was exhausted, mentally and physically.

But oh, I would like to see some of those fine people again: guests like Phillip Holland of Florida, who landed a thirty-pound salmon while angling with me in Bathtub Pool, and Dennis Duffy of Kansas City, who caught his first salmon on the Cains in October of '96. I would like to chat with Dennis Rice from New York; Nelson Bryant, an editor for the *New York Times*; and John Randolph, editor for the *Fly Fisherman* magazine. I would like to see Bruce Probert, a Maine forest ranger who called me "Professor" and whom I called "Superman" because he could cast a mile of fly line. (Bruce is the longest fly caster I have ever fished with, and that includes Ted Williams and Lee and Joan Wulff.) I still get his handwritten cards in the mail at Christmastime. He and his first wife Joan really appreciated my streamside teas. Just as in handwriting—a skill I am told is no longer taught in schools—you can judge a person's personality by the gracefulness with which they cast a fly line. And I thank God that there is no high technology to replace the feel and elegance of this art.

Golfer Jack Nicklaus and his wonderful wife, Barbara, fished with us too. And there was Annie Pearson of Massachusetts, whose mother died of a heart attack while angling this river when Annie herself was a young girl. Annie returned every year to fly cast these sacred waters until, in her late eighties, she passed away in her American home.

In high water, when the main Miramichi River was not fishable, we took our guests to the Renous, a tributary and early-run river that had its own rugged beauty. Or in the autumn, there were day trips to the Cains, a late-run feeder river where we had access to a private cabin and good water. There we lunched on the shore and George fried potatoes in a long-armed skillet, while our guests basked in the yellowing sunlight.

These men and women dressed in khaki. They smoked pipes and drank whisky. They were the last of the Hemingway and Faulkner mindset, the lovers, the romantics left from the waning twentieth century. They were the bullring, the boxing ring regulars, the Winchester rifle shooters, and the pursuers of big game. Some of them had fished with Lee Wulff on Newfoundland's Portland Creek in the forties and the Forteau River in Labrador in the fifties. Others had known and fished with Jack Hemingway. One man from Ketchum, Idaho, could recall seeing Ernest Hemingway—a bearded, frail, and old-looking man at age sixty—talking to himself as he wandered about the streets of that city not long before he died. These were accolades worth mentioning at the evening meal when the guests competed for one-upmanship in storytelling.

Some of these sportsmen and sportswomen would have belonged to the prestigious Anglers' Club of New York, a place where you needed to wear a sports jacket to get through the front door. Others belonged to lesser-known fishing and hunting clubs. Here too, they dressed the part—khaki pants and shirts—smoked, drank, and told stories about the places they had been to fish, which they compared for stature because it was considered a virtue to have travelled and fished well. The women hung out with the men, on and off the river. The Black Rapids Lodge with its flower-fringed, dreamy waters was designed for people like them. Their spirit is alive and well here, even now, as I write this.

Some of our clients left a last request to have their ashes scattered on these shores, as did Class One river guide Blake Sturgeon, who worked with us in the high summer when it was overly busy.

Yes, we still have a special place in the mind of our clientele. The few that are living—perhaps in seniors' homes—keep in touch with George as though he were a northern nephew or a grandson once removed. I get the occasional card on the anniversary of some event that I no longer remember. They are lonesome old voices now, shaky on landlines, perhaps at Thanksgiving or Christmastime. (No one ever lied about being lonely.) In their coherent moments, they nostalgically recall the good times: the river experiences sometimes confused with other rivers they had fished—so healing and melancholy—and they make arrangements to return to Black Rapids. They want to come back even now.

And George tells them, "Yes, come along! Welcome home boys and girls. Yes, come and fish with us again!" Again, we make plans to greet them.

There is a certain comfort for our old clients in hearing the river's voice and planning to return, however impossible the chances. Of course, there is no place for them to come to, as the operation has long since been sold to a big foreign concern from Alabama.

Still, they are welcomed to this sentimental place in our minds, even now, especially now, in the uncontrollable after-years, like a Patsy Cline song might take you back to a young romance. (For this stretch of water has become the place of old loves and old ghosts.)

Or maybe they are just walking down a city street and catch the scent of a wild rose or a cherry blossom. And for a brief moment they are back in this place and time, so fragile and yet so real for those of us who knew it and lived it. As if that old-world fragrance, more stable than an aging mind, has maintained its strong voice and carries in its smell the very best of old times.

So they make plans to come again and fish with us, asking, "What flies should I bring, which rods, what clothing will I need?"

Everything is scribbled on blank paper by trembling hands. But these fragile arrangements are perhaps forgotten in the next moment or lost in a dosage of much-needed medication, as happens with the elderly, before they are wheeled back to their respective bedrooms, where the now-fading and scrambled dreams live on like jerky strands of black-and-white film, caught up in the freeze-frames of long ago.

Dry Flies Made of Blossom

From the end of our hand-mown yard, all the way upriver to that big gully in back of the old Cavanaugh place, the field had been standing with timothy high as my head and purple with blossom. As long as that hayfield stood tall and solemn, crowding our farm building and line fences, the summer was still young with no end in sight. But now it would be a question of the weather as to when the hay would come down and be carted to the barn. The silage was ripe: when I pulled on the seeded blossom, the strands held together, bringing roots and all out of the ground. In their early or even half-ripe stages, these plants would have separated midway and the moist mid-stems were something to chew upon. They tasted sweet, like a cow's breath.

Of course, the field had been plowed the autumn before, one furrow at a time, not long after the cattle had been brought in off the aftergrass.

It seemed like only a week, the way time flies in summer, since my father planted the seed. He had carried in its harness a little cyclone seeder that, as he turned the crank and walked with a hurried gait, proceeded to broadcast the tiny kernels evenly into the freshly harrowed loam that was ankle-high on farm boots. This was after a week of harrowing at all the different angles, occasionally stooping to pick up a rock and chuck it into the trees without losing his stride. Sometimes he lifted a wing of the harrow to unclog its teeth from a build-up of switch grass that played hell with the drill making. After the seed was sown, the land was harrowed again with the lighter spike-teeth, and then gone over with the land-roller so that it looked like a field of dough, ready to be cut with a tumbler into molasses cookies. For him, it was a lot of walking behind horses.

I had walked behind my father in those harrowing days and gathered the angleworms to use for bait when I fished off our shore with a bamboo pole and a black fish-twine that my grandfather (Papa) had given me. I brought home big speckled trout and early cold-water chubs, and sometimes a gaspereau or shad for the frying pan. It was like unspoken teamwork; my father unconsciously offering up the bait, and me bringing home the supper fry. The same comparison might have been made later in the summer, when I took the timothy blossom for an army worm or a caterpillar and threaded it on my hook to make a dry fly, which I could cast into the choppy waters at the mouth of Morse Brook and raise a grilse, even a salmon, in the early mornings. These fish would hit at the blossom on impulse in the same way I have seen them strike at a bucktail bomber. In those days, our river, with its reflections of clouds and flowers, was loaded with yield.

By then, in midsummer, the bird cherries were ripe along the field's hedge groves, and I had gathered blueberries for the dinner pie. Near the riverbank, the John Deere mowing machine had been backed out of the shed and swung on its pole to stand like a tooth-laden monster. It grinned over the tops of the wind-blown timothy as if to say, "I'll have the last word with you." The mower's iron wheels clinked as the pole was lifted, and Father hitched the horses to the trace chains. Then he lowered the newly sharpened tooth-bar down to the half arm to bounce along until, at the edge of the crop land, it was dropped. Kicking the machine into gear, the matched team moved with a cluck of Father's tongue and a slap of reins. The mower chuckled and rattled as the timothy fell from its standing place—as if tripped by some grassroots underworld power—and were swept into a swath by the wooden mouldboard, which made wheel room for the next passage. The timothy lay in parallel rows with the spiked mower tracks separating them, smothered in places by the tangled red clover. Buttercups, dandelions, daisies, and devil's paintbrush lay withered on the ground.

This work was done in the early morning, before the heat of the day had begun and the blade of the mower and indeed the scythe—in places where the mower could not reach—cropped all the better. I can remember hearing the clanging of scythe stones and the clinking of the mower as it turned at the field's corners and struck out on another course around the perimeter of the flat, until that meadow of wildflowers—having been circled a hundred times—lay horizontal in thatches of greens, greys, yellows, and purples. Then the whole countryside looked bigger, having been crowded for so long by the stand of hay that, during windstorms, it looked like a multicoloured sea of rolling waves. The plants had grown without us having noticed a change in them. Some, though, had lodged due to the winds of thunderstorms, their stems buckling, to be used by nesting crows.

From my shared bed in our country house, and also from a cot on the open veranda where I sometimes slept on those short summer nights—it being too hot to close an eye in the slanted-ceiling, poorly ventilated upstairs—I heard the sound of the scythe stones, the mower, and my father shouting to the horses. These were the sounds of life on the farm. I found that out there, in the country, a change in the weather could renew a person's lease on life—a time when we had to adapt in harmony to the conditions laid out by the elements. Sometimes if the veranda cot was taken up by a brother or sister, I took my pillow and blanket to the yard where I slept in the hayrack on the wagon. It looked like a giant basket, open to the sky, the cannon-like spoked wheels around me standing on guard, waiting to be put into use. At such times, I was up and gone to the river by daybreak, my collection of the ripe blossoms to be used as dry flies.

And on those hot summer mornings, a grey haze hung over the river; the spruce trees on the other side were blue into the horizon. I rushed past the rib-toothed rake that stood hunchbacked in the yard. With the shafts pointing to the ground, it looked like a giant peacock with its tail feathers lifted in a spray—that or a woman's hoop-skirted dress, held up for safety as she ran. I hurried to the mouth of the brook to test the resting fish with timothy or a clover blossom.

I changed flies as the day brightened, changed blossoms to correspond with the shades of light and the shortening shadow, as the sun climbed into the clear sky. A strong scent of fish, water, and blossom permeated the air on mornings like that. Sometimes a salmon would move on impulse when one of those purple blossoms hit the water and skipped. Sometimes they grabbed the blossom and got hooked, and I struggled to bring them to shore, alone there in the morning sunlight with the shore grass up to my shoulders. These fish were filleted and then divided among neighbours who had come to help with the haying. There was always a heartfelt acceptance around me when I brought a fish up the hill to be filleted for the supper table. It was the warmest feeling of love I felt in the family circle. And this made me more eager to catch more fish.

After the hay had lain for a day in the sun, my father walked with a fork and tested the making. Then he raked the silage into windrows, our fastest horse trotting ahead of the big iron wheel rake to create a dust, scatter hayseed, and tear at the roots—expected to grow the next year—until the field lay in rows of hedges that looked like hurdles, or giant army worms heading in wavering rows toward the river to raise a salmon.

I can remember my grandfather, an old man then, lifting the hay and pitching it into bunches. And how the fork's handle bowed under the strain as I followed him with a wooden rake and picked up the straw that his fork had missed. For a while the field stood in pointed haycocks, each one raked down in a thatch that would ward off the heavy dew or even a light shower, to be shaken out the morning after to make in the sun and a breeze that also gave our line and garden trees a biblical voice. I sneezed throughout because I had hay fever.

There was great straining in the fork handle, too, when Papa pitched this crop into the rack, and my father stood on top to build the load, placing each forkful in a certain position so he would be able to read the build when he was pitching it off into the mow and not stand on hay he was trying to lift. We stood on tradition. A kind of wisdom came with the building of the load: if you remembered where each forkful was placed, it could be unloaded more easily. As the wagon crossed the field and Papa pitched on the giant bird's nests, and I raked behind him, my father used the prong of his fork to tweak the reins that had been tied to the rack's front post to keep the horses moving, this way or that.

Papa was hard-living and the strongest man in the world when he was young — he boasted that as a young man he could lift a cask of lime into an express wagon — but at the age of eighty-six in the fields, he sweated profusely and his fleece-lined lender top was soaked. He was wiping his face with a cotton handkerchief, also dripping. Until the last bunch of hay was loaded, I raked behind him and kept my wooden rake away from under the wheels of the big wagon. "Like a good boy." My sister brought us some cold water in a sweat-beaded galvanized pail, and we drank from different sides of a tin dipper.

Already there were storm clouds in the downriver sky.

The spirit of the moment, the need to get the hay in because we all knew our livelihood depended upon it happening that day, drew the family into a unified mindset, with the extended goodwill that makes a giver happy. It was a bonding that I loved and hoped would last. (This would return in a small measure with the potato harvest or gathering stove wood, though these tasks were not crowded into one fine day.)

Of course, after the haying was over, the bond was left to unravel (except mine on fish days), and we all went back to our separate, inner thoughts. There was no longer a need to unify our intentions, to harmonize, and the now-bigger fields lay in grey stubble, with the melancholy look of autumn, the sun having yellowed already from midsummer. Our internal feelings, scattering under purple sunsets, took us to dream of new places and new experiences we were eager to commence.

By then the fish had moved from the brook to the river bars and were looking for the autumn reds and oranges, as though the apples on our trees were now dictating the catches. Everything seemed related in the country of my boyhood: hay, apples, and fish.

Up to the barn doors, always propped open at that time of year, the rumble of horses' hooves sounded as their iron shoes drove into the planking, our strawberry roans labouring to pull the load, which looked like a thatched-roofed cottage from the homeland, onto the thrashing floor. The load brushed the mow and the cedar-shingled scaffold to give it a gold-polished shine, while bringing that sweet-scented fodder into the loft for the cows' and horses' winter feed.

It was all in a long day's work, that time in summer when the harmony, the sun, and breeze were just right. The fishing that had been squeezed into the early morning and late evening hours was a big part of it. Then the barn doors, two-storeys tall, were closed and buttoned to leave vertical cracks that reflected the sun's rays on the overloaded mow. And with such a stock of dry flies, I sorted out the most likely patterns that would bring home a salmon, as a chickadee offered its cheerful little voice for a season gone.

Having moved away without having left the land, metaphorically, and realizing that truth can sometimes be more important than fact, these are moments I now reflect upon when I revisit that old home place and time in my mind.

September

When I was a schoolboy, the big fall salmon runs came into our river toward the end of August. They swam past our farm in the thousands, like so many schools of gaspereau and shad in May and June. All through September and long after the angling season had closed on the first day of October—when the deer and partridge hunting season opened—the water was awake with salmon and grilse. There was a lot of excitement at that time of year, as the adults talked of fish barrels and nets, guns and ammunition, and deer-hunting trips on the Cains River—even though the angling season was open on that river, and still is, until October 15. (The later closing day has since become a law on the Main Southwest Miramichi as well.) Generally, we had caught our salting fish by late September, and while our community's men were into river guiding big time by then, the calls from the uplands—the honk of wild geese, the moans of the moose call, the bark of shotguns from the depths of our woods—were inviting us to new adventures.

On those late August and September days, after the hay had been cut and the chokecherries were withering to fall from the hedge grove, where blue jays gathered with their crisp, forlorn cries—I remember a frost-biting upriver wind that hastened our move back inside the main house. For we had been living since late May in the summer kitchen because we cooked on a wood stove, and having a fire in the shed kept the main house cool. And the sun was soft and yellowing against the maple-syrup-coloured river where those big fish were jumping in the old home pool.

The apples were red, as were the hawthorn berries along the pole-fenced lanes. The bone-dry bottomlands smelled of fresh-cut grain, ripe pigweed, and manure. These melancholy autumn fields had a sense of loneliness about them, framed by the wind-blown pines that whispered at the edge of the woods and dotted by the neglected hayricks yellowing under the afternoon sun nearer to the barn. We embraced the warm hours of the day, the last of a summer too brief, until the harvest moon rose against an inclement evening sky.

By then, the salmon were tinted brown — like the water — with orange and black spots. The males had a long hook on their lower jaw. It took a bigger fish to weigh ten pounds at that time of the year, as they had lost a lot of their sea fat and were approaching spawning time. But these leaner fish were best for the salt barrels, and this was the season when the river people collected their winter's food supply. It was that time, after the oat fields had been harvested, leaving parallel binder tracks from the iron wheels through the shiny yellow stubble. The potatoes were hacked from the ground to leave heaps of black stalks, like cocks of cow manure, with a rotten one or a too-small potato left here and there through the unearthed loam, where horse and drag-sled tracks looped, and where the cows came to feed — by then grazing on the aftergrass — and the crows, too.

After school and on weekends, we had gathered the potatoes in sacks of burlap to be carted to cellar bins by an aging though able farm horse. We listened to the vegetables tumble down the chutes to the cellar bins, like coins in a slot machine that would buy us a dinner, come winter. Yes, each bumping potato carried in its sound the promise of a hearty winter's meal, perhaps even Thanksgiving or Christmas dinner.

For excitement, and perhaps also to signal to the other farms that we had our vegetables in the cellar and the picking season was over, on a windless evening, we set fire to those potato and cornstalk piles to make a big smoke and fill the river valley with a sweet-smelling perfume. It was a kind of ritual to celebrate the harvest's end.

Then we went fishing for those big resident salmon that were always jumping in the stretch of river in front of our farmhouse. The slanting sun would make long shadows that projected the aspen and the maple trees onto the water, foliage that by then displayed countless shades of yellow, oranges, and reds. In the early fall, an evening haze came in mid-afternoon, not from the fires so much but the waning sun, carried by the soft upriver breeze. We made cast after cast at a hundred different angles and speeds and cranked in many fish, which my grandfather salted in casks.

In those days on the river, we used the big number four Grey Ghost flies and the catgut leaders we had to soak overnight before we attempted to splice them. Our rods were the hexagon-shaped, eight-foot, three-piece split bamboo sets with two tips made by Montague Sunbeam. Our reels were from J.W. Young or Medalist. This was the equipment we had always used to fill our salt barrels, to crank in those autumn salmon that were half our size. We leaned back on the rod's cork to apply pressure on the fish and eventually lead it over a waiting scoop net, until the barrel was filled and covered with salt, which drew the moisture out of the fish to make a brine that was as thick as pickle.

The barrels were filling with salmon, and the cellar bins were overflowing with potatoes and carrots and turnips. By this time, our mother and grandmother were into pickling and preserving berries and apples. Our minds had turned unwavering now to the uplands because the echo of rifles were repeating more and more, and so loud that we could hear them even from our schoolhouse while we were pretending to keep our minds on our lesson of the day. (I had ordered a Daisy Red Ryder air rifle from the Sears catalogue for $7.95.)

Our teacher, Mrs. Lillian M. Underwood—my father's sister—sensing we were not really into our studies, slammed the classroom door with a disgust that was followed by a deafening silence in the room. Mrs. Underwood was a no-nonsense educator, but of course her students felt more loathing toward her discipline than admiration for her intellect. She held this place in my thoughts until I was a grown man. I can still see her waxen face under a net that held her mixed-grey hair, and her below-the-knees dress hems and bulging Oxford shoes with the heels worn in a slant.

I also remember those cold, rainy fall days when the grey smoke of stovepipes settled in the valley and overpowered the fragrance of dead leaves, the barns' manure piles, and the unearthed potato lands. The smell of those chimneys hung over the river like an autumn fog. This aroma stayed with us even when we were in our beds at night or in our schoolrooms or when we were out on the river, casting from our old, homemade board boats. And you could tell what kind of stove wood—seasoned or green, hard- or softwood—a neighbour was burning by the smell of the smoke. For someone to be burning poplar firewood was a disgrace, cedar a sin.

⌒

Years later, when we were guiding for the big outfitters—for we were all river guides first and foremost—the late-September mornings were cold and the water in the ditches was covered with a paper-thin sheet of stained glass. We had to scrape the frost from our windshields with the backs of our pocket combs. Our old pickup trucks shimmied and rattled along the chip seal river roads to the camps where we were working long days. And the trucks' heaters, little rubber fans mounted on the dashboard, blew the hot air upon the windshield to make beaded patterns — like an artist's sketches of Mount Logan — that were erased in patches by faulty wiper blades.

On mornings like this, we put on many layers of clothes and then a raincoat over top. The raincoat served two purposes: to keep us dry against the upriver squalls and also to break the wind. At this time of the fall, we wore the raincoats even on sunny days. Unlike in summer when it is mostly tranquil, in autumn there was seldom a calm day; rather, these were brisk periods of sunshine or rain but always with that bitter, stiff wind that made the water choppy and mesmerizing. And we felt an aloneness because of the lost summer, the dreaded winter months that lay just ahead. But it was the time of year when we worked the river daily because the sports had come in droves, and having come from their city offices, it was the kind of weather they appeared to like best. Of course, the salmon were here in greater numbers, too.

For the guests, it had long since become a river of hook-and-release. For conservation reasons, this became a law for residents and non-residents alike. The fish had become more valuable as a fighter on the end of a line, as a tourist attraction, than another piece of meat in the frying pan. Anyone who thinks that this fish is worth more dead than alive is not a true river person, and probably has never worked a day on the river as a guide.

At the camp, once the guests had finished their breakfast — while we waited in the yard, standing and smoking cigarettes — we headed out along the river to whatever pool we decided to fish that morning, and we were always glad we had put on the fleece-lined long underwear and had crammed the second coat or sweater down inside our chest waders. We also tried to keep our feet out of the water — which is frigid, and our waders were leaky by this time of the season — except of course when it was necessary to help clients out to where they could cast to the salmon lies, or to help with bringing in a big fish. The fall dampness caused aches and pains and stiffness in our bones as we grew older. But the Americans wore the better, down-filled clothing that we could not afford.

Once the client got into position to wade down through the pool again in rotation, we guides went back to the shore and, in a sheltered place behind some big rocks or trees, built a small fire on the ground, using spruce limbs whenever possible because they make the better-smelling smoke. Half-filling a five-pound pail with brook water, we made tea for the guests and ourselves.

We all stood and drank tea, the sun warming our otherwise cold, wet rubber waders. For the sports, this was a welcome treat at mid-morning. We spiked the tea with brandy or Scotch whisky, which further heated up their veins and stimulated the circulation in their legs, as they danced and clapped their blood-red hands. I have yet to find a serious angler, young or old, who will not stop casting long enough to enjoy this treat, fish or no fish.

Because of my balance, or imbalance, I am not on the river so much anymore, not now, this far into the autumn of my own enfeebled years.

When my neighbours and I were younger adults, and night was falling on September Saturdays, we stole away from the river a bit early, washed up in the common galvanized boiler that stood on two chairs in the summer kitchen at this time of year, dressed in our best jeans, flannel shirts, and fine shoes—some wore gumboots—and got a lift on the back of a pulp truck to the village where a dance was happening in the Legion hall. Regardless of the weather, we went bare-headed.

We stood at the back of the big crowded room, glanced at one another's dress clothes while we listened to a cheap fiddle. And we drank from a flask that was openly passed around. Our strong lotions overpowered any rag-barrel odours that clung to us—but we could not detect—as a result of no indoor plumbing. It was such a common odour among country lads that it went unnoticed. Only the town people could detect it, and knowing this, we drew closer together so that all outlanders were equal in love and war. Though town people were better than country people: everyone knew that.

That rustic old fiddle filled the hall with the movement of happy feet. The women's sweet perfumes blended into a stew of roses and carnations, like at a wake house or even the whorehouses we had heard of in the city, but the aroma was overpowered by our want for love, though it also filled us with a lack of assuredness.

We each grabbed a partner and whooped and scuffed around on the oatmeal-sprinkled floor and swung the women, hooking elbows and tramping out the tunes played by a deplorable left-handed fiddler. The blind guitar player sang the waltzes about cheating hearts and lost loves. As we danced, the lads' Old Spice shaving lotion mixed with the women's more delicate perfumes. The scent of Chanel N°5 still takes me back there. Holding our partners in our arms, cheek-to-jowl we moved about the floor awkwardly, stepping on toes, bumping into other people like toys that had been assembled with a wheel missing.

The phrases from the Hank Williams's love song, the melancholy of which we had experienced ourselves—I could have written the song—brought a kind of dejection to the circumstance. The would-be lovers in our arms, the, oh-so-brief romance, it might have been an adolescent school play with the strong boyish undertone of shyness and indifference. Such was the inexperience of the days when we were young, and those village women filled us with solitary dreams, to give us a life and make our future complete, for a short while at least. (Until, having squeezed her too hard and for too long, she responded with a slap and a "You bastard!" and walked off the dance floor. We were left dejected and embarrassed. I still believe that the emotions we felt in our adolescence were the strongest of them all.)

Then, inevitably, a big fight started outside to crash the moment and fill the night with rage. The dance hall emptied to cries of, "Let me go. I'll kill that son-of-a-bitch!"

And it was the sharp-elbowed country lads — always troublesome and angry — who started the fight.

"What?"

"Let him go, Joe!"

The night was mostly over by then, except for the mouthing off and the name-calling. Soon we were walking or looking for a ride home without having held in our arms the woman we so desired. The fact that we were no closer to her spiritually at the dance than we were on the river, that she was equally obscure to us in both worlds, was a melancholy and desperate thought. Because everyone wants to enhance their station in life, even for a moment, especially a river guide whose expertise is so lonesome and deep-rooted. Nevertheless, great affection had been displayed, even in the fighting: the show of imperfections that demonstrated we were, if nothing else, consistent in the vitality that raged from the bottled energy we had shared before it was vomited or pissed away. And we were our old introverted selves again, feeling the emptiness that always comes with that badly played fiddle music, the taste and fumes of raw whisky.

At that time in Miramichi (the river), the dance hall was the centre of our universe, and we were actors on the world's stage, like the bigger-than-life scrapping heroes we had seen in the picture shows at the Uptown Theatre in Miramichi (the city). Afterwards, at home in bed, it was dark at the window. Tomorrow seemed weeks away. We were vaguely remembering how we got the sore jaw. We tossed and turned in a fit of half-sleep. Maybe it would go away with a good night's rest. Would the emotional scars be visible tomorrow? We tried to pass out, but our minds were tangled in a hundred little angers; water, maybe a drink of water, an Aspirin or two.

And then, suddenly, there was light at the window: tomorrow had arrived. Oh God! How could we get through this long day on the river? We were too old for this, yet we needed the money. We got up and looked at ourselves in the bureau's mirror to assess the swollen jaw, the hair growing white now. At this age, we should have known better.

Back on the river, early in the morning, we stood in the waist-high grass, slipping and sliding in the dew's moisture, dragging on a cigarette and coughing while nursing a severe headache.

A right arm was twisted out of joint from all the dancing and fighting, but we laughed at ourselves while smothering the shame, the sadness at how the night that started out with so much promise, but had come down so badly. Again.

At this time of the morning, the scent of the water, the over-ripened lupines and ragweed were strongest, but we did not smell them, because this fragrance was steeped into our clothing and our minds. Up the shore, a one-eyed dog barked, too loudly, possibly at a turtle or a snake in the grass. And from up on the hill, in the pens there were squealing pigs, soon to be killed, scalded, and hung by the heels in the open doors of threshing barns.

A church bell rang on the breeze, a church bell rang...

"Boys she's a cold, damp one, eh?"

"'Tis so, cold for September."

"But she was a hot old night in the village last night."

"Ha, haaa, what a circus!"

"Boys, what I'd give for a drink a black coffee."

"I'd like a drink of somethin' stronger meself."

"Young fella would you go get me a coffee..."

"You'll feel better after breakfast at noon."

"A little swig of mouthwash wouldn't hurt you either."

"Boys, don't anyone tell Mum about this!"

"Okey-doke."

"She'd be in church this s'mornin'."

Our jaws smarted, even throbbed from where we had gotten hit at the dance, a part of the late night that had become smothered by a haze. We had no desire to dig it up. The rosy scent of perfumed whisky and beer, tobacco and vomit—the graveyard breath of Sunday mornings.

"Did anyone see the bastard who hit me?"

"What?"

"Someone said that because of all the fighting and the big crowds on Main Street, the Fredericton bus had to detour around the back lane."

"Go on! That has got to be a record!"

And then the rain started in big slanting drops that swept up the river and hit the water like so many BB shots. They bounced off our raincoats and chest waders and put a grey sheen on the water, the shore grass, and rocks, so that it all seemed like one big wide river, and we were wading in it up to our necks. To try to escape from the loathsome morning it had become, we turned our backs to the river and closed our eyes. We tried to move, and then stayed, transfixed in the woman's presence, the woman we had danced with the night before, and we saw again her dress's V shape at her bosom, smelled her perfume, felt her silk in the rain.

Behind us the sport fishers fought the wind and rain. They swished their rods as if in anger against the sour-turning day. Their rods slapped the water, their lines tangled, and they barked at each other. But they were trying to compete with one another, to be the best fisher in any conditions, and to be mentioned in angling journals.

I hope he falls in, arse over teakettles, we think without saying it. We should be in church anyway. It is Sunday. God help us.

The guides looked at one another but said nothing. But anyone could read in their looks, "Yes, I wish he would fall in. We might get off the river a bit early if he got a scalding." While the rain hammers off their tin faces and iced-over glasses like slingshot rocks off a steel roof, we are too wet and cold to look at our watches that only serve to slow the day to a crawl because the morning has no fire, no hot drinks. So our minds shifted back to the women at the dance.

We stood in a kind of habitude, slouched down against the cold, like cattle that face one another, our backs to the wind and rain. We looked with one eye out from under our hoods. We all had only one eye. We rubbed our unshaven jaws, pock-marked now from the rain and the wind—like heavy raindrops in a sand hole—and we smelled the rank shore hay and the algae from along the water fences, the dead eelgrass that had caught up on the exposed rocks, having encircled them like winter scarves.

Finally, the rain stopped and a feeble and yellowing sun peeked over the hill to evaporate the fog and light up the water—with its drifting specks of foam—and started the fish moving so our unaware guests could get their day's catch and leave camp happy with a big tip for everyone.

Briefly, a faded rainbow appeared.

"Yes madam, the river is full of fish. But they are not showing at this hour. Yes, you are using the right fly hook."

"Am I reaching them?"

"Oh, yes, madam, since the rain and wind stopped, yes. You are casting well; graceful as a ballet dancer. The best caster I ever guided!"

A beaver swam across the eddy, slapped its tail, and went under to leave a circular wake.

"There's one," someone said.

"Yes sir. Right in close."

In the early fall, we fished and hunted woodcock and partridge in the uplands with an old Irish setter that was deaf and almost blind, but had a good nose. We got no birds but the outings were splendid experiences. We were young in the sixties and seventies, when the music was great. Peasant dresses, culottes, bell-bottoms, and double-breasted overcoats were fashionable in that day, shawls and long hair notwithstanding. We had no apprehension about any long-term future. It was that carefreeness I spoke about earlier that made the times so great. The river was always there, not only as a place of pleasure and meditation, but as a supporting arm for seasonal guiding, a much-needed income supplement.

In my maturing years, my ex-wife, Janet, and I worked the long days and weeks, making a living at various jobs in town and country. (I worked in a department store downtown and to make ends meet, took my holidays to guide in the spring and fall.) Through the summers with our young family, my wife and I took long weekends, driving a seven-passenger station wagon to some remote river, camping out and fishing with our boys. I remember canoeing the Cains River — an eight-hour run — with my three sons on a rainy day in September. We had eaten our lunch in a cave that was across the river from Herman Campbell's camp, which is just below where the hydro lines cross the river for the second time. Crowded into my old eighteen-foot Chestnut, we were singing as we paddled through Hells Gate rapids until the canoe struck a blind rock, and the boat was tossed sideways and almost capsized. We actually took in some water.

This scare brought us back to reality. Steven, only seven years old, was so frightened he wanted me to put him to shore so he could walk the rest of the way back to camp. But we were mostly through the rough water by then, so we relaxed and got our bearings. Still, for the rest of the three-mile journey, Steven lay on a cushion down on the ribs of the boat's belly and kept his eyes closed to the surroundings.

During those days, when life was happening, we were looking forward to the time when we could retire from guiding, get off the river altogether. We were waiting for the years when we could sit back at our river camps and watch the scene from picture windows with a glass of good brandy, a fire crackling in a stone fireplace, and a pot of hot, decaffeinated tea on the stove.

It is funny how after doing these things, the river guiding I mean, with the different clients for all those years, we wished away the days until quitting time, and now that we are free of the river, at least physically and financially, we will give anything to have those younger legs, keener vision, and that youthful carefreeness back again. Like old boxers, guides hate to give up the game, even though our legs are the first to weaken; then our eyesight blurs and balance falters. But oh, to be out there with those people from all over the world who we shared those special moments with. The river itself has stained us accordingly. And having guided for so long, we know no other occupations, no other reflections.

Sometimes we admit that we didn't realize how good the times were until years later. And we grasp backwards for some distant impressions that are no longer there, things that have since become enhanced by the illusion of nostalgia, so that we cannot even see them for what they actually were. In the mind it was something glorified, like a computer-enhanced photograph.

And the same is true of the fishers who will take a drink, enjoy a cigar or smoke a pipe, and while they are no longer smokers, we guides can still smell their rich American tobacco flavours that mixed so nicely with the drinks, the woodsmoke. These ephemeral things take us back to those special moments of river camaraderie, of sun, wind, and rain, and a good cup of spiked tea or camp coffee. And we can see the smiling faces of the wonderful people we worked with for so many years. They are here in the decaying weed and manure smells, the fading garden lands, and in the sounds of the trickling water that, because of the dampness, has a foam line this time of year.

Traditions are hard to maintain in this electronic world of screen-gazing. It takes a good river, a good sense of being to bring us back to an old reality. But I think that through the years, Septembers have been good times for me.

Fishing the Gray

Today I am guiding Paul Valeri and Jeff Mose, Connecticut anglers I have known for years. They are fishing that stretch of hard-to-wade open water on the south side of the Gray Rapids Pool. Known in fishing circles as The Gray, this is a long stretch of fast-moving water — the community's namesake — largely open to the public.

It is a cold day near the end of the season, and a hostile rain lashes up the river to penetrate my raincoat. The giant boulders and bank ledges appear to funnel the west wind into this canyon, and there is great turbulence on the river proper. Red maple leaves drift, half-submerged in the velvety froth. Here on sunny fall mornings, there is kind of hush — like summer Sundays on the farm — that lingers in the shade of trees, becoming more crisp in the breezy afternoons while casting a purple hue to the plowed fields. And in the evenings, we have the most spectacular sunsets in Canada. But at times like this, the sky is dull and spooky and there is the sour autumn smell of dead bracken, the spectacular foliage invisible to anglers who have their eyes trained on the moving water.

With my back to the storm, I am hunched down in my suit that has a rubber smell stronger than a half-smoked cigar. Standing on boulders — where as a kid I played hopscotch, holding one foot up, while hopping from rock to rock, getting to "Heaven" — I shout to my clients who have been fishing this stretch of river every autumn for as long as I can remember.

"Suppertime!" This is a word they do not want to hear, not yet. But I am shivering like a moon that dances on waves, and I crave a shot of single malt Scotch. Being old and native gives me a safe-conduct pass.

There are fish showing. In front of the camp, Jeff has waded into that deep hole where the water slows and big salmon stop for the afternoon before heading up through the run. They are stacked there like fish we see in aquariums or a fishbowl that has side mirrors. On fine days, they lie in the shadows of a cloud or a giant boulder. Today Jeff is making the long cast, at ninety-degree angles, using a pinch-barbed Ingalls Butterfly and the beaver stroke.

"Fish it by the inch," I holler. "Like dancing, it don't mean a thing if it ain't got that swing!"

Here, instinct goes further than intelligence, the bohemian crutch. I have used it for a hundred years. It comes with experience and is unexplainable, like trying to teach someone skywriting magic when you cannot do it yourself. Or perhaps it is like in a recurring dream where you grab at the coattail of a wonderful woman, one of the few things more important than fishing. Maybe the answer is in the sketches that the morning frost makes on the window panes. They dissolve from the heat after they reach their finest forms. For sure, it is a formula that needs concentration, even meditation. It is so fragile that if you talk about it or write about it too much, it will cease to exist. But everyone on the river knows that the first quarter of any hour is lucky, especially eleven in the morning and seven in the evening, those witching times of day when the water and air synchronize.

As time passes, I understand less and less about the behaviour of these fish and wonder if they can actually comprehend the long journeys set forth by one another. Or if it is all done from natural instinct, a following like when we chase subconsciously after a trendy fashion or, perhaps without thinking, the colour of the month. And I wonder if the fishers actually think that I know the answers.

Jeff has landed three salmon this day. I have watched from shore as he played those big fish that ran down into the wide river bend and leaped like the slow-motion tarpon we used to see on *The American Sportsman* television show. To a screech of the reel, the biggest one jumped, hung in the air and made miniature fountains, flapped and twisted in fits of vacillation, leaving doughnut-shaped wakes to widen and drift away. Jeff was holding it just short of a leader-breaking strain to make it leap six times before it began to tire. (Jumping fish will play out more quickly than sulkers.) Then it went deeper into the eddy, and I could see Jeff pulling up on the rod and reeling to keep the fish coming. The line was curved at an angle, out into the deep water, and he was trying to lift the fish to show me the tip of its broad rubbery tail. Then the big salmon came fast and circled in close, but was too deep and too fast-moving to tail.

He did this twice before I got my hands on the fish — just ahead of its tail — to cant it sideways. Keeping its head underwater, we took the hook from its jaw. Because the water was cold, the fish did not need much reviving and had plenty of energy to swim away. In warmer conditions, we would have held the fish so that it was facing into the moving water for as long as it took to get it to snap itself out of our hands.

"I never knew that you were such a good fisherman," I said to Jeff. Preoccupied with the moment, he did not respond.

In spite of the wind, there are great acoustics here. Now I blow on a blade of grass held between my palms to make a whistle. "Let's go!" Indeed, for me the day has turned from play to sacrifice. It is the price we pay for getting old and senile. (In a sense I have become a sentimentalist without illusions.) But I understand these men and their need to get on the water on this short fall holiday, because a river is the best of all healers.

I think of the April that I moved back home from Ontario: my brother Herbie and I fished all day in a snowstorm. And my mother served us warm soup in the cabin. We enjoyed every minute, or at least I did. There was so much "city" in my head, so much corrosion in my mind. I had to get back to nature, retreat to the river to feel whole again. And the bad weather made it all the more rugged, more of a challenge to light a cigarette, keep our hands warm. After some time, the woods and river, the old cabin, the birds and animals, and the fish took on my own personality, as before, and I looked upon these things as being a part of myself.

Behind me on the hillside this day is Paul's log cabin, a place he bought from Maine's Foster Gordon in the summer of '85. Before that, it had been the old Curtis sheep farm and then it was sold to Ted Williams of the Boston Red Sox. Later, Williams sold to Gordon and purchased a property in the community of Gray Rapids. Near the riverbank, he built a split-level home and called the place Fox Valley. It is now called White Birch. (I had gone there to fish with Ted Williams and his guide, Roy Curtis, many times during the seventies.)

Paul's camp is carousel-shaped, with a big stone fireplace, Hansel and Gretel curtains, patchwork quilts and a La-Z-Boy recliner beside the natural hardwood fire — so inviting on a day like this. And there is an aroma around this cabin: brewed coffee, delicious spaghetti and chili sauces, and single malt Scotches. It reminds me of my father's log cabin in the fall of '59, when the smell of woodsmoke was strongest on days of wind and rain. My cousins and I rolled our own tobacco, played the current hit parade tunes on a transistor radio, and shared a quart of Moosehead ale on Saturday night sleepovers.

There have been so many metaphorical streams in my lifetime, so many make-believe relatives to hug. I am a Yankees fan today and a Red Sox fan tomorrow. You have to be a diplomat.

Sometimes Steve Pomazi, a friend of mine and indeed a comrade to the Valeri camp—he lives in Fairfield County, Connecticut—drops in on his way back home from the Matapédia where he owns a lodge. In tow behind his SUV is his thirty-foot green Sharpe canoe, which we slide into the water and pole around, sometimes going down to the Black Rapids.

Steve is one of the most generous and classic men I know, a sentimentalist like myself; we have some great heart-to-heart conversations about the rivers in our souls and the seasons of life. Many times we made plans to canoe the Cains River together, but this has never happened because of low water conditions in that short fall window, and sometimes because of health issues, especially in my case. (We are both grey-haired old men by now.) And while Steve is in good health and robust, I believe the responsibility of a day-long river expedition would overtax my old mind and body.

Paul and Jeff have me here more as an icon than anything else. Now for something to do, I make tea in the thermos-shaped samovar that Paul has brought from the United States. I light some birchbark, and as it burns and makes a rank-smelling black smoke, I feed small sticks of driftwood under its bottom and drop a special decaffeinated tea bag into the boiling water. We gather around the steaming and hissing little pot and enjoy a cup of tea, spiked with brandy of course. Paul tells me that he has raised a salmon up in the bend at the top of the run.

Jeff has so much confidence in me as a guide that he says he will fish in the shore grass if I tell him to. Of course, he is a better angler than I ever was. Six feet tall and lean as a garden rake, he can throw a hundred feet of line with ease, even against the upriver wind. He grabbed onto that beaver stroke—which took me years to master— and perfected it in one morning's fishing. But I go on letting him think that I have some kind of special insight about the mindset of these fish. Why spoil a good thing. I never get this kind of respect around home.

Paul does not need a guide legally because he owns property (the cabin and panel-fenced hillside) and has a government exemption. Tony Velari, Paul's father (deceased in 2005 at age eighty-eight), had been fishing the Miramichi since the early fifties, when he stayed with Herman Campbell in Upper Blackville and was guided by Jack Sullivan. Paul had travelled with his father in those days, fishing the big river and the Cains, where Herman Campbell owned a cabin. They caught many fish, both father and son.

Following old footprints, it was for his dad that Paul bought this property in '85. Having grown up on this river, he has the same affection for the water and the life as I do. In honour of Tony's memory, Paul has founded a program titled First Cast MSA, which brings young people—especially Indigenous youths—to the world of fly-fishing. Paul comes to Doaktown's Atlantic Salmon Museum each summer to facilitate, while staying at his lodge here on The Gray, a fifteen-minute drive. All is free for the participants, including angling tips, equipment, and sharing information on access points where the public is welcome to fish. In six years, he has put through over one hundred attendants. Other volunteer facilitators in the program are local fly fishers Dewey Gillespie, Jim MacQuade, Vin Swazey, and Hilary Howes.

The Miramichi Youth Fly Fishing Program is a similar operation out of Miramichi Valley High School. This was founded in good part by local guide Jason Curtis and teacher Ashley Hallihan.

Right now, Paul is wading up on The Gauntlet. I can see him sawing away like a hunchback fiddler, under his hooded rain gear.

The stretch of river between there and the Doctors Island water, across from where I am standing, accommodates many anglers when the river is low and the long beach on the north side is exposed.

If that beach is under water, go elsewhere. Anyone will tell you.

⌒

When I started guiding legally in the fall of '61, it was to this pool, The Gray, that I brought my guests. I was working for Paul O'Hare, the pipe-smoking, New York–born Canadian who owned the Doctors Island camp in Blackville and, among five other pools, a good stretch of The Gray. My sports got many salmon here, some of which I roasted for them on open fires. Some of them liked my barbecued salmon so much that Paul O'Hare had me roast one for the evening meal back at the lodge. I stayed for the meal, ate the gourmet dishes, and drank the good New York wines.

It was a romantic old time when you could still hear a train whistle echoing along this river, a church bell clanging on the breeze, or the crack of a deer rifle from the wooded hillsides. It was a two-month-long hunting season in those days, and deer were plentiful, with the bag limit of two of any size, any gender. When we weren't guiding, we went to church on Sundays.

On the river I smoked the American cigarettes, took a shot of Scotch with the sports at lunchtime, and pined away my time through the long tiresome afternoons, thinking of my girlfriend—a hopeless passion—and how I might steal away a few minutes early, go to the Ross Diner in Blackville, and dance with her to an Elvis song on the big nickelodeon.

In those days, Ted Williams and his first wife (a tall blonde model) could be seen standing about in tackle shops like Doak's or Allen Brothers, or casting the long line in pools like The Swinging Bridge or The Gray. Lee and Joan Wulff were teaching river etiquette and fly casting at their place on the Beaverkill River in Lew Beach, New York. They visited here often. And there were rumours of Marilyn and Joe having stayed in a river camp near Blackville. For sure, it was a wonderful romantic, though simpler, time.

In the seventies, when I was writing for Tourism New Brunswick, Lee Wulff became a friend and mentor, sponsoring me in the Outdoor Writers Association of America. We knew all the same people, but from different sides of the aisle. Dr. John Losier, a dentist from Lyndhurst, New Jersey, became a friend for life, exchanging gifts and cards at Christmastime. Like the arts community, the fly-fishing family is a small circle.

Save for Joan Wulff, they are all gone now. The relationship with my first girlfriend, though always dubious and void of promise, was the first to fall apart. She moved on to better things after enrolling at a big university in the city. She took with her that inner future I had been nurturing. I imagined her pure soul being contaminated by the outside world—beyond me, beyond the village, beyond the river, and indeed her home province. I knew my hopes of true happiness would not be realized—as when a member of the family drops out of the circle, never to return—our old excitements having been destroyed by habit and the unsophisticated redundancies of down home. But a woman in the mind is all I really needed—and that is all she ever was, I guess. I wonder if she would even remember me now, or recognize the little old man I have become. I think that, if there were more people like her in the world, there would be more country love songs coming out of Nashville.

The older I get, the harder it is for me to recapture those abstract moments of long ago. But all are alive and well in spirit when I come to The Gray. It is like going back to reread a novel by Hemingway or Faulkner: you know how it ends, but you read it anyway because you believe it to be a classic.

At Duffy's Run

When the aspens were yellow, snow flurries were in the breeze, and the last wild goose was heading due south, Dennis Duffy and I contemplated a drive to Cains River, a fall-run salmon stream and a tributary to the Main Southwest Miramichi with its confluence at Howard, which is near my river camp. It was October 15, 1996, the last day of the angling season, and Dennis was still looking for his first Atlantic salmon, ever. Dennis, having arrived from Kansas City seven days before—he was staying at the Black Rapids Lodge where I was guiding—was eager for this day trip to a place that I had been bragging about, having spent so much time there in my youth, and which is a part of the old home lands where my great-grandmother Maggie Porter was born and lived until she married John L. Sullivan and moved to Barnettville, New Brunswick, in the winter of 1865. Her rock cellar can still be found on the river flats just below the mouth of Salmon Brook.

With his friends Tim Trabon (of the Trabon Group) and outdoorsman Pete Blair, Dennis—who lives just a stone's throw from Kearney, Missouri, where Jesse James is buried—had come to the Miramichi that fall to fly fish, but also to celebrate Pete's fiftieth anniversary as an angler and a field shooter at a Missouri sportsman's club. Peter Blair had been able to trace his lineage all the way back to George Washington. Tim had just returned to Missouri from having filmed a documentary on the Amazon River for Jacques Cousteau. In short, these Midwestern gentlemen were more American than apple pie.

They had planned this trip so they could catch a fall salmon, yes, but also to celebrate Thanksgiving Day in Canada for a change, and so Tim and Pete could chase some woodcock with their matching 16-gauge Parker shotguns. Since arriving, they had been fishing the home pools at the Black Rapids Lodge—which is in the Gray Rapids district (Route 118)—without success. Now with just one day left in camp, which was closing day, I suggested to Dennis that maybe he could try that old home water as an option because it was closer to the size of river he was used to fishing for browns and rainbow, streams like Spearfish Creek in the Black Hills of South Dakota and the Spring Creeks of Wyoming. And I knew he would like the storied, smaller Cains.

On the morning of Thanksgiving Saturday, I had Jean Curtis, the camp cook and camp owner George Curtis's wife, put together a lunch for us. We left early on what would be a cold and blustery day.

Having gotten the keys of the gate to that private area, I took Dennis to where George's brother-in-law, James Underhill, owned a cabin. From Upper Blackville (on Highway 8) it was down the Brophy Road (a sandy one-lane trucking route), out a long, rocky wood trail, and over a big red pine summit to the river. James's camp sat on a bluff overlooking the water, which appeared black as tar as it wound its way through the yellow shore grass and orange aspen wilderness. Fellow river guides had told me that many salmon had been taken on this stretch throughout that fall, but it had been vacated this day because of the foul weather.

The Cains is a barren-fed, slow-moving tributary that lures the novice canoeist because of its gentle gait and that which can be reached across with a long spey cast. Its coffee-coloured waters tint the main stream for miles below its confluence, which is why we use

the amber-tinted German leaders. Dennis fell in love with the place at first glance.

It was close to the host camp in Gray Rapids—less than one hour's drive over paved and good gravel roads—yet it was like we were in a different country. For sure, the Cains River had its own atmosphere and spirit and offered its own melancholy state of mind.

Dennis and I unloaded our grip on the riverbank in front of James's cabin and walked to the top of the pool, picking our way through alders, around and over flat and beaver-shaped boulders. And there were bears, barrels, and SUVs of black granite we had to navigate around. Dennis waded in to his thighs and started working the cast on his way down through that long stretch. He was using a fly hook called the Chief Needabah, which was made of red and orange feathers tied on a number four hook, a Cains River favourite against the dark water in late season.

In the distance, a raven squawked—the sure sign of a storm. Dennis wanted to know what kind of bird it was. I told him this bird —a member of the crow family—had a broad vocabulary, offering a different sound for various weather conditions. And it also responded to discrete calls. I had once fished with a Mohawk man who talked to the ravens: using a "shriek cry," he called one up to our fire site.

Around the bend, upstream from us, was a stretch of fast water— on what was really a slow-moving stream—between the old Brophy place and the Teedlin place, and then it slowed to a crawl as it meandered through a spartan autumn landscape, down toward Hells Gate Rapids, a good half-mile-long stretch. But we could hear the rapids, loud in the pre-storm air, so filled with echoes. On the far hillside, Bill Hooper, a retired forest ranger and biologist from Fredericton, had a camp. With its pole veranda facing the river, it looked like Robert Service's cabin in the Klondike.

The old Teedlin place had once been a family farm in the mid-1800s, where, according to river guide George Hennessy Sr., a black bear came out of a grove of cedar one spring night and stole their young pig from its pen. It was a place where, in season, you could have stood in the front yard and called a moose. As a teenager, my father, wearing his Sunday clothes, walked to the old Brophy place on Saturday nights to play cards — a good eight miles from our farm at Keenan — with his contemporaries John, Joe, and Jerry Brophy. And he would be asked to sing a little song for Mr. Brophy and his wife, Cynthia, contemporaries of my grandparents. Sometimes my father rode there on horseback, having crossed the main river on the ferry at Howard or perhaps on the bushed river ice in winter. He saw moose, lynx, and bobcats along that road, too. He called it the "old" Brophy place even then, though the family still lived in the grey-shingled farmhouse with its front veranda facing the back hillside. It was as if, like its neighbouring farms, the place's fate had already been determined, and there was a feeling of impermanence about the setting, even then.

Eighty years later, frail and suffering from dementia, my father would sing those old hobo and cowboy songs to his fellow patients at a long-term senior care facility in Quarryville, New Brunswick. The memories of his youth had all but diminished, but he remembered the songs.

I can recall feeling a similar sense of remoteness when, in the early fifties, my family took a Sunday drive to visit my father's older brother, Silas, who lived further up the Cains River on his small farm. It was near Shinnickburn where there had been a schoolhouse and the possibility of a new church. Silas and his wife, Margaret, had gone there and carved a decent livelihood out of a heavy wood. (Although at the time, when it came to remoteness, there was not that much difference between Shinnickburn on the Cains and Keenan on the

Main Southwest Miramichi — the railway and hydro lines being the only difference.) Silas and Margaret raised a large family and were independent as the wind. They lived on home-grown vegetables, caught fish and wild game. That day, Silas showed us around his fields and barns — there were moose antlers on the walls inside his woodshed — and I can remember how my grandfather marvelled at what Silas had achieved, having left home after his wedding in the thirties with the inheritance of a young horse, an express wagon, a single-furrow plow, a .45-70 Winchester rifle, and a firm handshake from Papa.

Silas and his family lived on Cains River until 1960, when he and Margaret abandoned their youthful dream and moved out to Upper Blackville, on the main river, where a high school and a doctor were more accessible, the roads paved. They purchased the Herb Morehouse place, a farmhouse and former country inn for railway travellers, and from there the youngest sons, Thomas and Darwin, attended Blackville High School. Years later, when Margaret and Silas had passed on, the Morehouse place was also abandoned — though kept in the family — as the siblings looked for more fertile grounds in cities anywhere between Nova Scotia and British Colombia.

They all became successful in the bigger centres, but looked back upon their early life on the Cains with a sense of innocence and longing for the old home place, where they had been so close to the land, the trees, and the great river.

The Miramichi and the Cains were that kind of wilderness farm country back then. In fact, the whole Miramichi River system had once been settled, farm against farm, fields joining fields that fronted the river, all the way from Howard to Wildcat on the Cains — at least twenty-five miles — and the full length of the Main Southwest Miramichi (and its other tributaries) from Bay Du Vin to Clearwater to Juniper, a good two hundred and twenty miles long. This kind of abandonment is still going on along the main river and the less remote tributaries as young people move to the bigger centres to find employment and a social life, the farming existence having disappeared decades ago.

Of course, when Dennis Duffy and I went to the Cains, it was a total wilderness: only a few ghosts remained at places like Brophy or Teedlin or Porter, where you might have found a house's rock foundation, a wild apple tree, black-eyed Susans, a purple-stemmed raspberry bush, or perhaps heard the forlorn cry of a Canada jay, that signature bird on wilderness farms.

Now as Dennis stood up to his waist in water and fished down through the stretch, I paced back and forth on the shore, shouting instructions to him—when to go deeper, where to step back—because the water was so black he could not see the bottom. I felt he could have stepped in a hole and gone over his waders if he was not careful. I was also suggesting when to cast at a different angle, a different fly hook perhaps, when to give it the beaver stroke, and so on. But it was hard for Dennis to throw a straight line against those black upriver winds; hence, the smaller wind-broken river on a day like this. On the main river, the big Southwest Miramichi, it would have been impossible to cast a fly line. In fact, Dennis's travelling buddies, Tim and Pete, had gone bird hunting, which in the noisy gales was also a hopeless venture.

Dennis and I were chilled to the bone as we stood in our fleece-lined underwear, fleeced-lined trousers, wool sweaters, and fingerless woollen gloves under the rain gear. Once Dennis did slip and go under, just for a second. He got an arm and one shoulder wet. I offered him a dry sweater from my packsack. He refused it, saying the scent and feel of the water made the river all the more intimate and brought him closer, philosophically, to what he was trying to achieve. (That

was a new technique for me.) By noon, a few big, wet snowflakes descended, one by one, from the low sky. Dennis fished that whole stretch, moving by the inch, and casting the angled lines across the ointment-like water, giving it a stroke here, a mend there, all the way down to James's cabin. And by then, with a too-short leader tip, the big number four Chief was hitting the water like a .22 bullet.

Above the cabin in the bend, there was a beaver lodge at the edge of a big eddy. And from the wind, a tall poplar tree came crashing down into the water—it had been partially chopped off by beavers— missing Dennis by only a few feet.

We heard gun shots in the distant woods. Some people were canoeing, fishing salmon, or hunting grouse and woodcock along those hard-to-climb pine tree summits.

In front of us, a few fish were jumping, but it being so close to the spawning season, the salmon did not show themselves that much. When Dennis finally came to shore to take a break, he was cold and stiff from standing in water that was only one or two degrees above freezing. His face was red from the sharp, cold New Brunswick air and from the iced tea he had been standing in. I left him with a shot of his own bourbon while I went up on the riverbank in front of James's cabin, and in the lee of the big spruce trees, built a fire and made tea. In the damp river air, the white spruce limbs burned orange and the pitch-smelling smoke, sweet as honey, blew low over the water. To warm ourselves, we drank tea and bourbon from the smoking porcelain mugs and exercised our legs and arms by pacing the hillside and shadow-boxing.

Then we sat by the fire to prepare our lunch. We were behind the low-limbed spruce to shelter ourselves in the alcove against the river's chill. From the ten-minute-boiled river water, I made more tea, which Dennis spiked with bourbon, and then I roasted the steaks Jean had sent, along with the hashbrown potatoes and homemade

Lady Ashburnham pickles and bread, with pumpkin pie, the traditional Thanksgiving dessert. It was a wonderful, tasty meal, made more appetizing because of the harshness of the day and place. The after-dinner brandy that Dennis had brought from Kearney, Missouri, set us into a talking and laughing mood.

We talked about Ernest Hemingway's days as a journalist with the *Kansas City Star*. And we talked of Jesse and Frank James, the Dalton Gang and the trains they had held up and the banks they had robbed in Kansas City. And of Mr. Howard, who had shot Jesse down. It was all right there in Dennis's mind, flowing out like water from a hose. And he promised to send me — on loan — a book on the James brothers and the Dalton Gang, a hardback he had had since he was a boy playing cowboy in Missouri, as I had done in the fields and woods around Keenan, New Brunswick.

Some moose-birds — said to be spirits of old woods people — glided in to grab bread crumbs from out of our hands, then fly away and hide them in the trees. My thoughts wandered off after them.

Indeed, while we were eating, the snow started to come down with more authority and the wind picked up. After lunch there was no time to recline and sip tea, or smoke a mini-cigar, because I did not like the look of the sky. When we went back up to the pool, there were already patches of white on the shores, and the big flat rocks on the hillside were white, the straw sheaves of shore hay projecting as if from out of the arms of scarecrows. Against the snowy shores, the water looked purple. It was like one of those raw autumn days that I could remember from my boyhood, when I worked in the woods with my father as he got up the winter's firewood. Every dry stick we gathered had a sense of warmth and the image of a hearth fire in it.

Despite the snow coming down, this time Dennis fished through the lower end. And finally I looked out to see him lifting his rod to

make it bow double, and I heard him shout, "Fish on!" He was arsing himself backwards toward the shore.

When the fish jumped, I gave him a nod and the two thumbs up. He had hooked into one of those big, fall-run hook-bills, brown as a boot and with the orange and black speckles along its sides. The big male salmon had made no wake, grabbed the Chief under the water, and immediately started on a long run downstream to make the Orvis reel screech as Dennis backed in to shore, without falling, and tried to swing the fish around to pick up some of the line.

But those old fall salmon are as tough as Sabbies River slabs, and I knew Dennis would have his hands full for a long time. We walked downstream along the shore as Dennis stumbled and cranked in an attempt to regain line that was still well out into the backing. Then the salmon jumped closer, showing his actual size (about twelve pounds), and made a run upriver, leaving a big belly of orange line slanting down and out into the acrylic water. Finally, when Dennis had the casting line retrieved and the short leader was showing above the water's surface, the fish circled and came toward me as I stood at the water's edge, looking to tail it.

With Polaroid glasses, I could see down into the water but a few inches as I followed the slant of the cutting leader. Once I had to duck under the line. I knew the salmon was tiring, as it was by then swimming closer to the surface, the tip of its shark-like tail visible. When it finally broke water after two or three attempts, with Dennis leading it in my direction, I got my hands around its body back near the tail, flipped it over, and lifted it up on the rocky shore. We took the barbless hook out and Dennis released the big fish back into the stream—without a photograph—after giving the salmon a kiss and then holding it underwater, facing into the currents, until it had regained all of its strength. It swam off with a scoot, back into midstream. This was easier to do in the fall when the water and the air were both cold and there was plenty of oxygen for reviving a fish that size.

Dennis's first Atlantic salmon.

It took a big hook-bill to weigh twelve pounds at that time of the year. I had seen so many photographs of fall fish. All had exaggerated poundage.

The shore was white with snow by then, as we washed our hands in the river, and the walking had become slippery as we made our way back to the more cheerful fire site, where there was still some warm tea in the pail. I knew we had to get moving, and fast, because the day had really darkened down: the sky was like slate, and the wind with the driving snow was coming fast and mesmerizing, like when you shake a snowglobe paperweight. We had a good fifteen miles to drive on those greasy roads, up and over the big hills that would take us out to the main river. On those steep inclines, there were cannon-ball-sized rocks. Others were watermelons, and some were pumpkins, half-covered and greased with a cushion of dead leaves and now snow. My car had smooth tires, and with Dennis and the luggage in, it was low to the ground.

I drove slowly as the storm had overtaken the gathering darkness. But soon we were on the pavement of Highway 8, proceeding slowly behind a transport truck that was spraying grey slush. We were heading northeast toward the lodge. Snowflakes dazzled in the lights of approaching vehicles, making it difficult to see. It was Saturday night by then, and as we drove through the village of Blackville, cars and mud-splattered pickup trucks were parked along the road, the open doors of the dance hall blasting its light and its country music into Main Street.

Since the lower end of the pool we had just fished—between the Brophy place and the Teedlin place—had no known name, we decided to call it Duffy's Run, after Dennis, and also in memory of the great day we had had fishing that stretch of the Cains. After we got back to the lodge, we stood outside in the falling snow with the other guests. Tim and Pete drank to our idea. We exchanged farewells, and I headed back to my own cabin, the long day's guiding a success, the season over.

Dennis Duffy still lives in Kansas City, although he has come home to our river many times since, without the same success. He came again in the fall of 2001, and he and I were on the main river during the disaster at New York's World Trade Center. Due to a late-summer drought, the Cains was so low and bony that fall, it had been closed to angling. We could only go there for a photograph and a cup of tea in weather that was too hot for comfort.

Fearing a closed border after the terrorist attack, Dennis had to leave camp in the middle of the night with a friend, Georgia's Larry Kennedy—who was also in camp—to head back home. Dennis stayed one night in a McAuley Convent as a guest of the Sisters of Mercy—they did his laundry—and then later with his Jesuit uncle, who was chaplain in Merion Station, Pennsylvania.

Dennis is now battling cancer, a dreaded disease that has since taken our friend Tim Trabon to the great rivers in the sky. And we all have the male prostate problems that come with aging. But I always get a phone call from Dennis on closing day, October 15. We reminisce about that wonderful trip at Duffy's Run that had so much character. It stays in our minds like an old love that we have no desire to let go of.

I hope that the powers above will give Dennis and Peter the strength and courage to come back to this second home, fish with us again. Because Cains River still rolls on as it has for eons, past the overgrown farmsteads, the big snow-covered rocks, the projecting sheaves of straw—depending on the season—and the overhanging pine trees. The smouldering fire site and that leaping salmon are still prominent in Dennis's memories, and mine, so much a part of our day at Duffy's Run.

The Sabbies

REFLECTIONS IN THE WATER

It is mid-October and I am fishing the Mill Pool on the Sabbies River. This is a tributary to the Cains, its confluence being two miles above Cold Brook—where my grandfather had a lumbering camp in the twenties and thirties—and a half mile up this little river from Stanton, which is at the forks. In the fall, on the old Mill Road below this pool, my grandfather and his boys used to ford the river with the horses and wagon to get to the long-abandoned McLaughlin place. (When this river is summer-low, you can cross it there with a pickup truck.) They hunted caribou and moose in those hard-to-reach princess pine woods. My father told me that while they were crossing the Sabbies, a half-dozen salmon got caught up in the spokes of the wagon and kicked into the box.

And once, after hunting in those woods through two days of heavy rain, they were unable to get back across a river that was bank-high and rushing past in brown leaping torrents. They waited in the abandoned McLaughlin farmhouse an extra three days, eating partridge stew and wild cranberries, before the river receded and the horses and wagon were able to ford back to the mill side. Even then it was touch-and-go, with Papa wading to his waist, leading the horses by their bridles, while the water pushed the wagon sideways. For a brief moment, Papa was down under and then he was up again, holding the bridle ring, his clothes clinging to him like the feathers on a scalded hen.

The Sabbies was a good salmon river in those days. Still is.

On this bright sunny morning, the river is shaded by the big trees on the hill where my car is parked. The water is dark and sullen, and there are small patches of froth drifting on the surface, with half-submerged red and yellow leaves scattered in the currents. Staff in hand, I am using a wide-legged shuffle to wade knee-deep upon a black, algae-covered riverbed. The fish are rolling deep in the still-warm water, yesterday's sun having scorched the earth with a new seasonal high, although this morning there had been frost on my windshield and it was minus seven degrees at the parking place. I have fished on colder mornings, fall and spring.

From up on that hill, the little river looked like a splatter of ink among grey, trunk-size boulders; the protruding alders, pen strokes at the water's edge. Having had two rises or near rises — the movements were very deep — I know there are fish in the pool. I change my fly-hook from a Chief Needabah, a size four red-and-yellow-feathered hook, to a smaller Copper Killer and give it some hand action. As in the Cains, these red and coppered fly hooks are what the salmon rise for in this bog-stained fall water.

I know I should have waited until the sun hit the river's surface, the water and air equalized, and the foam evaporated. But I am here for old-time's sake as much as anything. When I was a kid, I did everything in the early mornings. Now, such places and moments are on my bucket list to be relived and enjoyed at these specific places and times. I guess it comes from somewhere in the subconscious. I've long since realized that when we get elderly, we recycle things we enjoyed in childhood, so that even the old imaginings we used to get pleasure from are rehashed. And with our memories fading, quite often the dreams and reality blend together to become an alternate truth more real than the facts, the heart having overtaken the mind for a touch of grandeur, even romance. It is a kind of replay effect that comes in spurts from out of the archives of the heart. Some fragments come, no doubt, from the daydreams I sleepwalked through in my little country schoolroom at Keenan. I meditated through the crisp autumn afternoons, knowing my father and grandfather were up here, perhaps on a hunting or fishing expedition. Sometimes I tell these stories as if they were true.

In school, I learned that this is the place where Francis Peabody (founder of Chatham, New Brunswick, now a part of the City of Miramichi) built a mill in 1821. This was just four years before the Great Miramichi Fire of October 1825. That fire destroyed most of the ancient pine trees that were being chopped down and stream-driven to the shipyards in Newcastle and Chatham to be used as masts for the Royal Navy's tall ships. It is said that Lord Nelson got his masts here for the Battle of Trafalgar. (There is a community named Nelson further down the Main Southwest Miramichi.) In the early 1800s, Peabody sawed lumber for many of the homes that were built along our river and its tributaries. My great-aunt Sarah Nutbeam's house, still standing, was constructed from the Sabbies River plank.

There were not many environmental rules in those days, and Peabody dumped his slabs, sawdust, and other refuse into the river. These slabs drifted downstream, and many of them sunk. After two hundred years, they can still be found lying on the river's bottom as far down as Blackville and White Rapids, a good twenty-odd miles away.

When my father was fighting a spring salmon on the line in the heavy waters of April — or even eating a fried black salmon steak at the supper table — he used to say, "This fish is tougher than a Sabbies River slab. And probably was in the river just as long."

Now as I cast, there are the echoing reports of shotguns in the yellow morning. I think of another autumn when I was twelve years old, and I came here with my father, my older brother Winston, and our uncle Eldon to hunt deer. There had been a grey-board, broken-backed camp up on the hill where the parking lot now stands. That was where we stayed for all three days of the Thanksgiving weekend, having come up that muddy Mill Road from Howard after crowding into the cab of Eldon's '48 Dodge half-ton.

We got no game on those early morning walks, but saw many deer along the old portage route and in the alder-infested fields of abandoned farms. My brother shot some partridge with the .22 Ranger, a weapon he was old enough to carry on a minor's licence. I wore Winston's old made-over plaid coat, that had been too small for him but was much too loose for my thin arms, and my cowboy hat, a Christmas gift (which I always wore—because it was red—when hunting partridge in the alder swamps around home). Though ragged and patched, that was the warmest coat I ever wore.

Back then, on fall Saturday mornings, I hunted with a slingshot I had made from a bicycle tube, an even maple crutch, and a pouch fashioned from the tongue of a discarded shoe. I collected marble-sized rocks from along the railway line, filling my pockets until they chafed my legs. In the swamps, I stalked partridge that ran on the dead leaves and sometimes roosted well up in the limbs. I had to be careful and approach them from the rear, so they could not see my shots coming. I got many partridge, and these were cleaned and soaked overnight in salt water before my mother put them into a stew with vegetables; she was one of the greatest cooks on Earth. The birch partridge were the best tasting as their meat was white, like a domestic hen's; the little spruce hens were dark and wild tasting. The spruce grouse were tame and a bit stupid, and knowing their taste was not great, I walked past them. Even now, when I see a partridge in the woods, I talk to them—the old game bird of my boyhood—recalling a time when I sat in the schoolroom on Friday afternoons, the partridge hunt on my mind. Back then even a red squirrel was considered fair game. I got ten cents for them from the fly-tiers. Funny how we grow away from our childhood guilelessness. Today I would not kill anything bigger than a mosquito.

⌒

On the aforementioned Thanksgiving weekend, before dawn, in that tar-papered, lamp-lit cabin, the men fried pork and eggs. I can still see my uncle Eldon, down on one knee as he fed sticks into the stove's firebox, hear the clatter of the dipper in the galvanized water pail as he had wakened early to light the fire and make tea. I can hear the kettle hissing on the wood-burning stove, the gurgle and pop of fresh pork frying in the long-handled skillet, and smell the kerosene horse lantern that hung on a nail above the table. Using the clanging tin mugs, my father poured tea and sweetened it with molasses. It was first bitter, then sweet, and then oversweet.

"Just like in the old days, eh, Eldon," he said. "Like when we were logging with Papa on Cold Brook."

"What?"

"Like the old days on Cold Brook!"

The men reminisced — they were always reminiscing about one fall in particular — when they were youths and had come here to cut logs with their father. They had partitioned off an abandoned horse hovel and lived in one end of it, with the four horses in the other end, behind poles that had been caulked with moss from the forest floor. The men related how the smell of horse manure seemed steeped into everything, even their straw bunks and the potatoes they ate. They spoke of how their sister, Ida, came to work with them because she was being bullied in the schoolyard.

Ida worked extra hard, doing the cooking and cleaning as well as shovelling out the hovel and buck-sawing stove wood that had been cut during a long wet spell. (That wood never dried before it froze and had to be dehydrated in the big woodbox behind the camp's stove). She carried water in heavy wooden buckets for a half-mile from a spring and kept both ends of the camp spotless. It was hard work for a twelve-year-old girl who refused to go back to school. She seemed to be glad to be accepted here and would do more than her share of work just to be an equal member of the family.

When the woods operation was over in the spring of '28, Ida left home by train with our family's blessings. She went to Houlton, Maine, where she made a good life for a time before coming back to marry a man from Lockstead, which is near home.

Daddy recalled, "We always had Maine to fall back on when the picking season came. Ben Vickers and I went to Maine one time, and we worked all fall picking potatoes. Then hitchhiking home, we slept in old barns, were awakened by roosters—they stood on beams over our heads—their droppings hitting Ben in the face, and got a free meal here and there at farmhouses along the road." This was during his hobo and singing days.

"Yes, I can remember when you came home needing a haircut, and with your boots worn out," Eldon said.

"I made it better in Maine than we did on Cold Brook," Daddy said.

"Yes, we got twenty-five cents a log," Eldon said.

"For Gibson."

"And Snowball. He was no better."

"With the old cross-cut saw."

"And the double bit axes, Wilfred filing. Yes, and fiddling."

Uncle Eldon smoked tobacco after breakfast, as we waited for good daylight. It was a pleasure to watch him sitting in his flannel shirt, rolling a cigarette, the tobacco pouch dangling by its string from his teeth, striking a kitchen match with his thumbnail to light up, shaking the flame out before breaking the stick between his thumb and forefinger, and tossing it into the stove. How he enjoyed the tobacco's satisfying taste, with the cigarette slanting across his chin as he blinked from the smoke. When he was finished smoking, he opened the cabin's board door and snapped the butt-end out into the tall weeds with their brown blossoms still clinging to their stems. The smell of burning tobacco — though I encounter it more and more seldom — still takes me back to that special place and time. I can smell it here, even now on the river, as the memories come and go like dreams through a night's poor rest. I suppose such moments from youth, our own and our family's, will linger in the subconscious through eternity.

On that trip we ate partridge stew each evening, and after supper we sat at the board table and played a four-hander of Auction Forty-Fives. The men talked about how, in their younger days, on the weekends, they went to the dances in Howard and Keenan in Papa's new '28 Chevy. And they joked about my father singing at house parties in Doaktown and Gray Rapids, the country songs of Jimmie Rodgers and Wilf Carter being enjoyed by a hundred people.

"We drank the home brew that Francis Vickers and I made out in the swamp. Oh yes, those were the good old days," Daddy said.

"You were never a great singer, I never thought."

"But I could yodel."

"Everyone thought it was okay, I guess."

"Yes, them was the days!"

And I tell myself, the memory is likely better than the life really was.

As I recall, there were a great many salmon in the Mill Pool that Thanksgiving weekend: my brother and I saw them splashing about. The big moving schools made deep waves as the fish milled about and waited — we supposed — for a rise in water so they could move on upstream. We had come to the river with a dipper and a galvanized pail to fetch water to make tea, wash up in the mornings, and also to add some fluid to the truck's radiator that had boiled over on the Salmon Brook Hill on the way into the shooting woods.

"By cripes, he's no slouch," Eldon had said of me when I brought in the heavy pail of water just before dark.

And my father had responded, "He's the Lone Ranger."

These men were always joking with one another, and with the big cousinhood of nieces and nephews as well. But they maintained a distinct art of keeping their distance when it came to people outside our family circle. Meeting a new acquaintance, they would gaze into their eyes, long and hard, before shaking hands. And it never seemed to be about what they said; it was more about what had been excluded from the conversation that they were judged by.

At night, we said our prayers and father blew out the lantern. We got into our straw bunks, the upper one having a pole railing that, with the straw thatch hanging down, made it look like a miniature barn loft. In the black silence, the stove seemed much louder, the snap and crack of the burning wood, the creek and rattle of the stovepipes. I put my head under the covers. I was afraid of what might come out of such darkness. I was feeling the eyes of my dead uncle, Jack Underwood.

Yes, there was a ghost here on the Sabbies, too. For a long time I would not come to the river alone, not even in the daylight. Or if I came here and heard something strange in the trees or in the water, I ran back up the hill at about a hundred miles an hour. Like all country children, I was superstitious. I had good reason to be.

⌣⌐

Two years before, in April of '53, my uncle Jack Underwood had been killed on Sabbies River, not far from this place where we had set up camp to hunt. He was hit on the head by a log falling from a high landing site. In a scow, the log drivers ferried his remains down the river to the Cains and on down that bigger river to Howard, where an undertaker waited to take his corpse to the morgue in Blackville for a wake and big military funeral. Uncle Jack had served in the First World War.

I was in grade four that spring, and I can remember news of the United Church minister going to the school in Blissfield in the middle of the day to tell Aunt Lillian the news. Our school at Keenan, where Aunt Lillian had taught for so many years, was also closed. I remember the two-week-long holiday that followed, which was so filled with darkness. A spooky atmosphere surrounded the high-moving river with its logs drifting past—we wondered which one had killed Uncle Jack—and our little community for a long time after.

Pretty soon after the funeral, Aunt Lillian arrived with two cardboard suitcases filled with teacher's smocks and books. She had come back home to live, and there was no music, except hymns, no radio shows allowed at our house for a long time, especially the westerns that my brothers, sister, and I enjoyed so much. Instead, we got church services. She had been living just up the road on the next farm, a plot of land she had inherited from my grandfather—a house to which she would never return.

Perhaps unfairly, I have always associated Sabbies River with that early spring of high emotion, darkness, and superstitions. Oh, the horror of that illogical old day, that dark little river. It might have come from out of a Joseph Conrad novel.

⌒

Many years later, when my son Jason was a teenager, he used to come to the Mill Pool in June to fish for trout. Knowing the hatches and the scientific side of angling, he caught many big sea-run brookies. (He released everything and still does. As a matter of fact, for the last thirty-odd years, ours has been a hook-and-release family.) On that day, however, when Jason finished angling and went back to the truck, he found its battery had gone dead. His first thought was that of the ghost. In the middle of nowhere, he had no choice but to walk all the way out—over ten miles of gravel road—to Howard. There he called for his brother Jeff to pick him up at the house of Jim Colford and take him back to give the vehicle a boost. It was a long walk in chest waders on a hot June day. And some people actually drove past him on the road. It was a lesson for my family and me to not dress at home when going to fish, but rather to throw our wading boots and vests into the vehicle and put them on when we got to the pool.

Up the Sabbies a few miles from the old mill site, in the higher country, the river branches into two small streams: the East Sabbies and the West Sabbies. These little rivers are not much bigger than some of the brown trout streams we see advertised in New England's fishing magazines. Where the road crosses these rivers, there are picnic tables and rock fire sites for the weekend hiker and angler to make camp.

Later in the fall when the waters rise, salmon will go by the hundreds up these small streams. They wait at the river's mouth, just as they wait in the Miramichi for the right conditions to come into the Cains. At that time of year, in good swimming conditions, these Cains River fish ascend the Sabbies, Salmon Brook, Six Mile, and others, and on the main river tributaries such as the Bartholomew River, McKenzie and Morse Brooks, Burnt Land, Taxes River, Rocky Brook, Clearwater, Burnt Hill, and a hundred other feeder streams of the greater Miramichi River system.

Now as the sun clears the hill, the shadows shorten, and the foam evaporates from the water's surface, I start to raise fish and I actually get a strike. I know these are what my father used to refer to as "old fish," harder to raise than a Sabbies River slab. So I walk up the hill to the parking lot, get into my car, and drive out the Mill Road to the Half Way Spring, where I build a fire on the ground and make some molasses-sweetened tea, feed the moose-birds a part of my lunch before heading back. I think that it has been a good morning, though in large part recycled.

On Morse Brook

My first encounter with the spirit of Morse Brook was during the Christmas holidays when I was ten years old. Father had been cutting pulpwood alone, back on the south side of that frozen stream that was hard to reach, except in winter. I felt that working in the woods with him for a few days would be a great experience. Having heard so many stories about that part of our property and livelihood, I wanted to go there, share in the excitement. In addition, it would allow me to make some pocket money, get me into the picture shows in the village on Saturday nights.

In the late fall before — when salmon were spawning by the thousands in that stream — my father had gone to Newcastle and into a hardware store, where he bought my brother and me each a small axe. They were not much bigger than hatchets, really, but these working tools had been sharpened by Grandfather on the grindstone, as I poured on water and turned the crank, to grind their edges from heel to toe and back to heel, until they had a smooth-cutting though wire-like edge. And then he used the whetstone to give them a final spit polish. These kinds of work-driven occupations consumed me from childhood until I was eighteen years old. I was too far from town to be involved in organized sports, and my influences were my father, mother, grandparents, and a few positive-thinking uncles and aunts. These people remain my mentors to this day, though all of them are long dead.

In the early dawn of those winter mornings, dressed in heavy coats, wool caps, and hand-knitted mittens, my brother Winston, two years older than me, and I walked with Father well over a mile from our farmhouse into the woods, past a big spring that never froze over — its water was so cold it would make your teeth ache, even in summertime — down a steep hill and up the brook on the snow-covered ice to the work area. Squirrel tracks, rabbit tracks, and sunken deer and moose prints criss-crossed the trail. I looked for animals along the way. With my short legs, I had to struggle to reach Daddy's big footprints. As I laboured along behind Winston, a dark breeze sent a powdery frost sifting down from the tree branches to take my breath away. It made my nose leak and my ears sting from frostbite. I hugged myself.

I figured that, like a toy one gets in early childhood that is soon outgrown, my first impressions of the brook and wood were likely the ones I would tire of most quickly. I had pictured it all so commonplace, so dark and lifeless, especially in the winter. This was long before I realized that a stream and a wood have a spirit and a soul of their own, my young mind being too immature to sense it at the time. It would be some years before I could actually see it for what it really was, grasp and savour it as a place of freedom, a setting in which to create, to meditate, and to heal from the turmoil of life. In the modern day, this is sometimes described as "forest bathing."

These pulp logs were being cut and stacked for scaling on the bank of the brook. Their ends were stamped with orange or green paint, to be sorted at the boom by means of a colour code after they were stream driven in the spring.

While Father worked with the bucksaw and axe, cutting down the grey-trunked fir trees and sawing them into four-foot lengths, Winston and I chopped off the green limbs and the tops and piled those for burning. While Daddy had thrown off his heavy coat and was working up a sweat under a flannel shirt, my brother and I had to hop around to keep our feet from freezing.

"Daddy, I'm cold! My feet and ears are numb." I wanted to cry but was afraid my tears would freeze.

Daddy showed only a workman's indifference to our misery. He shouted at us, "Keep moving boys, don't be lazy," even though it was twenty degrees below zero, especially because it was twenty-below zero.

The frozen brook was as wide as a two-lane highway, and at the edges there were alder bushes, around which the ice was frozen, protruding out from the shores and up through the frosted glass-like covering, like a collection of charcoal sketches on a sheet of white paper. In places, if we scraped away the snow with our boots, we could see down through the ice to the amber gravel bottom. There was a beaver dam we had to climb over and scuff across what would have been a good skating rink had it been handy to home. But here with its snow covering, it looked like a giant white goatskin spread out among the black alders of the flat.

As the bitter cold morning wore on, and my father worked with the axe and saw, I stamped my feet as I waited for him to build a fire and make tea at lunchtime. I believe this was hurried somewhat when he saw that I was in such misery. He had not wanted me to come to the woods anyway, due to the risk of my falling ill and missing more school time: back then, I was plagued with insufferable asthma attacks. I can remember when I was just three years old—February 9, 1946—and fighting for my breath, Mother dressed me in a sailor's suit, stood me on the back doorstep, and took my photograph. She told me decades later that she did this because she was afraid I would not live through the winter.

Finally, Daddy chopped some pitchwood from a princess pine stub and, striking a kitchen match with his thumb, set it to burn. The strong-smelling, eye-stinging black smoke—so clear in my mind's eye even now as I write this—curled through the limbs above us as it took on a mind of its own and was no longer powered by my father's torch. Winston went to the spring to get some water for tea. Behind us on the hillside, in what my father described as a "var thicket," the tall young trees, some bent, some twisted, stood close together as though they were having a meeting, perhaps planning a conspiracy against the axemen. I wondered how an animal with antlers, or even a person with a blade, could get through such a close-knit copse.

At the fireside, as we consumed our baked beans, sandwiches, and homemade doughnuts with molasses-sweetened tea from Daddy's packsack, he told us how to determine which way north was by the shape of the trees and by the moss that had gathered in the limbs. And how all the tree branches appeared to slant toward the afternoon sunlight in the west. There was a certain ambience among those green treetops, especially when the breeze whispered through the needles as through a screen door: it carried the spirit of spring and summer around our old back porch. He told us about a time when he was a young boy working on the other side of the brook with *his* father, and how during an autumn lunch when a cold breeze was coming up the brook, a big hollow princess pine stub, loaded with pitch on the west side, burst into flame. The fire had been built too near to what he called a "rampike," and all they could do was move their lunch implements, stand back, and watch it burn.

"As the smoke and flame came out of the top, away up in the sky, it was like a chimney fire," he said. "Until the stub collapsed, burning even as it struck the brook with a hiss, a splash, and a big puff of grey smoke."

We had finished eating our lunches, using Mum's homemade bread to mop up our tin plates. After sipping tea from enamel mugs, my brother and I gathered the freshly cut fir boughs and tops and stoked the fire to make a great snapping and crackling sound, warming our hands and faces and sending flames and white smoke billowing up through the black limbs into the sunny, clear windless sky. In the bareness of the winter's afternoon, the snow reflected orange around the fire site, coppering our faces like the one we see on coins. And for many miles away, anyone could have spotted our signal. It became a kind of game we played, to see how much smoke we *could* make. I can still smell, even taste, a perfume from the burning balsam. It seeped into our clothing and remained there even when we went back to school a week later.

In the classroom, these wood scents came and went in shifting pockets: the rich fragrance of burning fir boughs that carried in its aroma memories of the holidays, the scenes of my father labouring on, and the cackles of a cock-of-the-woods, that million-dollar bird that roosted near our lunch site and hammered away on a hollow tree trunk. (I wrote an essay about woodpeckers for my teacher, who wanted to know how the class had spent our Christmas holidays.) These familiar smells and sounds still take me to that time and place, rekindle the authority of my father's words as he attempted to teach us the ways of the woods, while the big red-headed woodpecker, more voice than bird, is the intonation of youth, of Morse Brook, and of good times.

We worked with Father through the cold, late afternoons, even on stormy days when the falling snow clung to our wool coats to make them look like fleece. The wind gave the great oak trees, with their clinging copper leaves, a haunting desolate voice, the brook's meadows buried under a foot of snow. Tired, we headed homewards in the semi-darkness, for we had farm chores to do in the way of milking cows, feeding hens, and filling the kitchen wood boxes. At bedtime, finally, in the upstairs hall my brother and I knelt beside our shared bed and said our prayers, naming and blessing the whole family, one by one.

In the spring when the pulpwood was sold, Father gave Win and me each a crisp ten-dollar bill. This was a burgundy paper note that had a portrait of King George VI in the centre, with some fancy scrolls around his handsome face. In his high-collared royal tunic with the medals and braids, he had been younger looking on the bill and on coins than any pictures we had seen of him in the newspapers at the time of his death, or from earlier still, when he stood beside Queen Elizabeth in 1939, a long-feathered cap in his hand. Until his death, this portrait stared down on us from a gilded frame in our living room. The king appeared to be on the verge of speaking.

Somewhere in my childhood, too, during those dreary days in late autumn when the woods were grey with raindrops and perhaps a few snow flurries were scattered in the wind, my father, dressed in red, took his walk back to the brook, a 43 German Mauser tucked under his arm. And using an Indian deer call as an attraction, he brought home a giant buck to be admired by the community men as it hung in the open doors of our threshing barn and then was butchered for the salt cask. Father was an animal lover as I am, but venison, like salmon, was a necessary part of our livelihood. He was the best deer hunter I ever knew, though he never hunted for the sport and it grieved him to take an animal's life. When times got better and we were not so poor, the spirit went out of the hunt for Daddy, and he hung up the Mauser for keeps.

I recall as well, from my pre-school days, watching my father and grandfather getting ready to go to the woods on those cold, early winter mornings. They had packed a big wicker basket of food: homemade breads, beans, and molasses, with fried pork chops. My father went to the barn, harnessed the mare (her name was Maud) and brought her and the sleigh around to the kitchen door to where Papa—in his heavy leather moccasins, sheepskin jumper, and fur cap—carried the basket out and put it in a box behind the straw-tufted seat.

I shouted from the doorway, "Papa! Papa!"

"What? What's that?" He was hard of hearing at that point.

"Bring me home a Christmas tree!"

"You bet young fella."

He came over and gave me a jab with his leather mitten before climbing into the sleigh. He pulled a buffalo robe over their knees, Papa having sat shoulder to shoulder with my father, who with a click of his tongue and a slap of the reins on Maud's rump started her trotting across the big fields and over the old railway line, with its weather-beaten telegraph poles and insulators that looked like two scoops of lime-flavoured ice cream. They passed the bowed-down birch trees that stood along pasture fences, on toward the back gate and the woods. I stood in the yard and waved until the squeak of the runners, the pounding of horse's hooves, and the harness bells grew faint, and they were almost out of sight. Then I ran inside and upstairs to the empty spare room, and scraping the frost from the window, put my nose against the glass to catch a last glimpse of them, the mare trotting along the fenced lane and across that rocky, hand-mown buckwheat patch, small dark figures in a snowfield with its protruding yellow grass visible along the sagging rail fences. I could see that Maud was frisky in spite of the fact that she had foaled just four months before. At the edge of the field, the darkness of the forest soon overtook them, and they disappeared from sight. At noon time, when the sun was at its highest, I could picture them back on the brook, hunched like beavers by a little fire, eating lunch. These images appear to me now like scenes from out a Russian novel by Sergei Aksakov.

After the brief early winter day, when darkness was approaching, I stood again at the same upstairs window, staring at the edge of the woods for the first glimpse of the horse that would be puffing steam as she trotted toward home, my father and grandfather two shadowy figures sitting on the sleigh seat with the magical-scented fir tree that would brighten our home and bring gifts and neighbours to visit in the season that lay ahead.

Finally, at 4:45 p.m., when the table lamps were already lit, I saw them coming across the top hill, Papa and Daddy hunched like shadows behind the mare's smoking breath. I could hear the harness bells, mellow at first, the bang of the runners that were pitching and sliding as they crossed the tracks, the gathering December darkness bringing into concert the sleigh's musical harness. At the sight of home, the barn and house, as we used to see them from the railway, the trotting mare was kicking up chunks of frozen snow that struck the sleigh's dashboard like gravel stones, and her mane was blowing like a lady's scarf, the squealing colt in the stall waiting to nurse.

At the back door, Father stopped the horse, and Papa threw off a small fir tree.

"There ya go, laddie,' he said. "A Christmas tree for ya."

The little fir hit the snow-packed dooryard with a sigh and a flap of wing-like branches. It was not a well-shaped or a full tree; rather, it was open and sparse, but it appeared humble and self-deprecating. Still, because it had been Papa's choice and I admired him, I loved the tree on sight. Suddenly I could picture it there in the woods, standing among millions of trees, all of equal value, still breathing in its youth and growth. Then I could see it in our living room, being over-decorated with tinsel. And I was sorry its life had been cut off for my selfish desires. Of course, we always had a real Christmas tree in those days.

"Ta, ta, Papa, it's gorgeous! Where did you get it?"

"We got it in a clearing by the brook, just another little tree among thousands."

Papa was never one to expose his inner feelings. But I had an image of him wading through knee-deep snow, using the bucksaw frame as a cane, his legs tiring after a hard day's work. These were his last days in that wood because he was by then an old man, stooped at the waist, with unruly white hair that protruded from under his big fur cap.

That evening in our parlour, because he was celebrating his birthday, December 10, 1870, Papa played "Home Sweet Home" on his concertina. In his big work boots he got up and danced, and my grandmother laughed until she cried.

"Mammy," he said, "bring me another little taste of that brandy." I can remember how the music from the sleigh bells and later from my grandfather's small accordion lifted me into a happy state of mind, which lasted throughout the long winter's night and into the days ahead.

My grandfather worked in the woods until he was eighty-eight years old.

In my earliest boyhood, my love for the woods was Platonic in that I had never been in it. I had an image of the place that was really quite unlike the one I would get to know so well through my lifetime. Back then, I had associated the woods with shadows of lost trails and of wild beasts (wolves and bears) to be wary of. These illusions were almost sinister, like the radio shows of Mark Trail, Jack London, and Sergeant Preston. Years later, even blindfolded I could find my way through those forested hills, and some of this was because of the smells of the pitch in certain trees, the ground berry and hawthorn blossoms and the bracken in the different seasons. And I came to look upon all woods creatures as friends. Even now, in this wood and brook, these scents and sounds bring moments of my childhood vividly back to me. I grasp for that old magic like an aged man tries to recapture youthful delight, perhaps in the scent of cherry blossoms or the sounds of songbirds—which, of course, is unattainable because of time and one's philosophic growth, in the way that the woman one truly loved in adolescence always appears the more remote.

As a teen, I had a girlfriend in the village whose favour I was trying to win. I had taken her ears of corn from our big country garden, as well as some potato soup. My mother scolded me for pursuing a high-bred townie.

I said to her many times, "Mum, she is my true and only love."

In that early winter I was in bed with pneumonia, and a doctor had been out to our place to give me a needle and warn me against going to the shed for stove wood or to the spring for water. But it was a time when my lover's father had taken a stroke and was partially paralyzed. Not knowing I was ill, she called to ask if I would go with her to our woods to get her family a Christmas tree. Heedless of the doctor's orders, I got dressed and, taking the axe, went with her to Morse Brook. We brought home a small fir tree. She had worn a long black winter coat and a pale green bandana that draped like a bonnet around her black curly hair. Never among schoolmates, choir girls, or restaurant waitresses had I seen anyone so beautiful. Plus she was the most level-headed and smartest person I ever knew, indeed, a great influence.

On the way back to our farmhouse, as we dragged the tree, she was filled with energy and, with a sparkle in her eyes, sang a Christmas ditty. This lifted my self-esteem to new heights, and for a brief moment I felt like I was a part of her family. But I was overtired and delusional and having sat down to rest, thought I might faint. Still, I was joyful for the fact that we had shared this experience, because she told me that she would be moving on to the city, to the big school come spring.

"We do not receive wisdom, we must discover it for ourselves," so collegiate, she had paraphrased Marcel Proust. Through the years, any-one who formed a distinct likeness to that young woman—however subtle—attracted me. But there would be no similarities when it came to movements of the heart. And I wondered how small a place in her mind I occupied, or if I was ever there at all.

Sixty-odd years hence, on a sunny fall day, we returned to that place, sat by the brook, and shared a cup of tea. Two old people, with our lives behind us, reliving a special moment by virtue of recollection. After she was gone, I took the mild-scented napkin she had used at fireside, folded it, and put it in the top drawer of my dining-room cupboard.

But what I was going to say before sentiment broke in with truth about my first love is, until that grade four Christmas holiday, I had not been to the brook when it was running open. Of course, I had seen its inky waters tumbling beyond the guardrail as it flowed under the plank bridge where I walked, my sister and I, to and from our little school at Keenan. Actually in April when it was in peak flow, the chuckle of the brook, black as tar, could be heard, even seen, from the windows of the schoolroom. Many times when I stood for the readings or the singing of "O Canada" and "God Save the King," I thought about throwing a baited hook into those turbulent waters. But after my experience with Father and Winston, even years later when I was driving across the bridge on my bike and later in my old man's pickup truck, the sight and smell of Morse Brook always took me back to that former time. The water carried in its music the simplicity of the day, my boyish infatuations with the stream and wood, and its beckoning draw to solitude.

⌒

In the winters that followed, father cut logs along the brook and made landings as big as our barns. In April, the logs were rolled into the stream and driven a few miles down, under the school bridge and railway trestle, to the Main Southwest Miramichi River, from where the were taken over by the corporation crews to be rafted down the big river to the boom in Millerton.

I can still see those log drivers with their high hobnail boots, broad hats, and their prancing white horses as they pulled the lumber, which had been left on flats when the stream dropped, to the moving water. They rolled them down the bank like pork barrels, and they struck the river with a spray of white foam. Actually, I measured the logs' worth by the size of the splash they made. The men walked along the shores — some were adrift in scows — like gypsies and whooped and sang the shanty songs that were unfit for a little boy's ears: "Oh here we come we're full of rum . . ."

I can recall too, at that time, on a sunny Saturday morning in April, up the brook near Snakes Spring, Winston and his friend Ralph Campbell built a raft out of cedar logs. They had a plan to sail down the brook to the highway bridge. Congested with asthma as I was — an environmental allergy that doctors had not found a cure for — I wanted to go, even if it cost me my life. But, of course, they would not take me along.

It was a good raft and when launched, it floated high on the water. As I watched them from the hillside, I was vexed that they would not let me go on this great adventure. But I hid my indifference to their high spirits and grudgingly displayed a happy face.

The sun was warming, and there was a rustling of treetops as they pushed off at the Upper Landing and stood tall on the raft, stepping this way and that, striking the water with long poles to keep their balance, as the catamaran swung into the currents between the shore alders. Things were going well, and the Huckleberry chums drifted along without incident — until, I am told, they came around a sharp bend where a long windfall tree was hanging low across the stream. This swept them off the fast-moving raft and into the dangerous waters. My brother, not being able to swim, hung on to the tree branches until Ralph, who had swam to shore, got back out and rescued him. I remember the two youths coming home, wet and chilled to the bone.

In the fields there had been a cold breeze—smelling of the bare ground and top manure—that tossed the river elms so they looked like big, leafless brooms sweeping the sky. This made the stovepipes rattle and creak as Win and Ralph stood behind our kitchen range, hugging the pipe, absorbing its heat, while my mother fed them hot drinks and scolded them for attempting to do such a dangerous thing. Shamelessly, I was hard-pressed to hide any hint of my innocent pleasure at the failure of a plan that did not include me.

Later that summer, Father took Win and me back to the brook to fish trout. We walked that same trail to the big spring, and this time the ferns and bracken were up to my chest. There were summer birds singing and crickets and mosquitoes buzzing around me. Daddy told me the names of the many flowers and berry bushes that blossomed along the hillside. These were the images that would last longest: maybe I had grown enough to appreciate them by that time. The woods seemed to be full of life as I stumbled along, chewing on a blade of grass. The outlet from the spring, well-sunken in the moss, was tumbling down the hill in a series of miniature waterfalls, which made freshet sounds and sparkled like a tin dipper pouring hot stainless steel liquids against the forest floor. We stood on our heads to get a taste of the stinging cold water that was always such a treat. And there were tea berries, moss berries, strawberries, and the half-grown blueberries to snack on. While it was a hot June day, it was beautiful there at the spring with the low-hanging, soft fir branches and a cushion of cool moss under my bare feet.

Without wading boots, my father and Winston rolled up their pant legs and stepped into the stream—at summer low, it was up to their knees—and waded down the centre, two abreast, their hands with the rods reaching before them like diviners. I walked along the shore, among the alders, stepping into bog holes and decaying patches of frog spawn that stuck between my toes. Some of the flowering plants were as high as my head. And once I cut an index finger on a razor-sharp fern. To stop the bleeding, I held it in the brook until my father bandaged it with his handkerchief.

They fished the water ahead of them with baited hooks and six-foot-long leaders, eyes anxious, for a good mile down past the Devil's Elbow where the brook was narrow and deep on one side, and the trout came out from under a pine root to snap at their hooks, then on down to Aunt Edith's Hole — named after our great-aunt in Minnesota — which was a big whirlpool partially covered with froth.

It was not easy for me to follow them along those alder flats. Once in a while, one of them caught a pan-sized trout and tossed it to shore for me to scramble and catch before it got lost in the undergrowth. I strung the fish on an alder branch to be brought home for a breakfast fry. At the whirlpool, Daddy gave me his fishing rod, and I cast out to get my first small trout ever, a fish that I quickly tossed back into the water — because it was struggling for breath — and watched as it scooted away, over the washed amber gravel.

And in the originality of those first boyhood days in that wood — where I would occasionally hear the far-off whistle of a passing train or the knell of a church spire, muted by the whisper of a breeze in pine needles, the chuckle of water — I found a great cohesion, even mysticism from the outside world, the stream giving new meaning to the voiceless words *blood of the land*. This served only to intensify the pleasure of being where I was, in a landscape filled with wildlife and plant life in all its forms. I was on Morse Brook.

On Morse Brook

I know my father had fished this brook with his father when he was a boy, back in the days when the trout were bigger and more plentiful, the waters larger and colder. Papa told me that using a duck-feathered (red) fly hook he tied himself, he caught a two-pound hook-bill speckled trout in Aunt Edith's Hole. And my grandfather had fished the brook with his father, just as his father had done with his father, and so on. Indeed, we had been living on, working on, and fishing these waters for more than two centuries.

But the days when my first forebears came to Canada are a long time ago. And these ancestors appear to me now like characters from a Dickens novel. They are blotted tintype photographs kept in a drawer under the piano bench. They look a bit like Papa, but are bigger, with exaggerated features, longer beards, and seem more able. In the photos, they stand among their sheep and dogs somewhere in the hills of northern England—that so-called "purple land" of W.H. Hudsons—and then later here on our New Brunswick farm, and indeed Morse Brook. They sleep in a village graveyard at Holy Trinity Anglican Church, a vine-clad Thomas Hardy–style chapel with a four-pronged belfry. Each summer, my brothers, sister, and I make our pilgrimage to visit their graves. For sure, they have fallen to dust more quickly in their burial places than in our hearts.

Like my ancestors, I have long since learned the value of a wood and a stream as a place to meditate and to pray. My father had been living in this mindset all his adult life. Toward the end, his leisured and partially demented mind, became fully occupied with recollections of his youth. Father had never looked upon the woods and brook as a place of entertainment or even commerce; rather, it was a sanctuary, an abode more sacred than life, an escape that became even more consecrated in memory than it had been in real life, in the way that time and distance enhance a thing. In his declining years, he stood before an easel and painted the old wood and brook scenes: the lunch site, the log drive, the fishing prospect. Until, nearing death, his power of recollection and indeed expression had vanished from his sentimental soul and the landscape and brook perspective was out of all proportion. But in the words of Anton Chekhov, "There is nothing in our lives that does not end sooner or later."

Still, the traditions are engrained to be passed down to the next generation. And it has become a bone of contention among siblings over who has acquired my father's best hangings.

When my father died in June 2005, my brothers, sister, and I dug his grave, as for Papa, and we were his coffin bearers. It was only then I learned that I had inherited a section of the woods and the stream, and this is where, when I am gone, my ashes will be scattered. To me, it is more sacred than the village churchyard. In my will, this place will be passed down to my sons, and hopefully to their sons or daughters. Through the years, my own young family and I have fished this brook annually on Victoria Day, which is in the third week of May, for our once-a-year breakfast fry.

Now as a senior citizen, I see my middle-aged sons taking their families to the brook on this spring holiday weekend. And the boys marvel when they feel a strike, see the flash of a fish's belly in those purple spring waters — experiences to be remembered later in life. They can see that each tree has its own expression, as do the vales and meadows under a certain light, the rambling, spirited stream, free-flowing. We talk about things related to the wood and brook, stuff that makes sense only to ourselves, as we recount every trail, spring, and tree on the property. And about a stream that comes out of the undergrowth with the solidity of a piece of artwork, to gurgle around a bend and loose itself in byways of dreams.

Certainly, through the generations, we have all drank the same spring water and fought the same generations-old mosquitoes and blackflies, broke the same alders to carry the latest progeny of this inherent trout. And this has become a rite of passage for us all.

For we are from an old landlocked English family, standing strong in a place where few of our annual traditions prevail. And we refuse to sacrifice this outing, this place, for any new world order or screen, any virtual reality or cyberspace that we know cannot replace the natural image, the togetherness and the good times that the woods and stream carry in our veins. I believe there are some things that technology cannot improve upon and are better left the way they are. A wood and sparkling stream can be a beautiful place on a hot summer's day.

And in winter time as well. They will care for me while I sleep.

Afterword
THE MOOSE-BIRD

My father was a lover of birds. Even around our farmhouse when he saw a hen walking, he would pick it up, stroke its feathers, and look into its sparkling eyes.

He would say, "Come here, Wayne, see the pupils, the beautiful colours, the passion." I remember the hen's eyes as being traumatized; not from my father for sure, but from humans in general, and the chopping block. Still, my old man claimed that—as with our dog—he could learn a lot about the nature of any species by looking into its eyes. He told me that as a boy, he looked into the eyes of a fox he had caught in a snare. In the woods, when he came upon this animal that was being held by the foot, he stroked its head and back—like anyone might do to a dog—and looked into its sad and bleeding eyes, a dangerous thing to do. Then he took the snare from the animal's foot, and set it free. The fox ran away and he never saw it again. Nor did he ever set another snare. While in his younger days he hunted deer for the winter's food, I never knew my father to kill a small animal or a bird. But he would have loved to have had them as pets.

He told me that when he was a young man working with his father in the spruce woods near Morse Brook, each day when they built a fire to make tea and have lunch, the moose-bird (Canada jay) glided down on silent wings—as if from out of the smoke—to gather their bread crumbs, and carry them away to hide in the forked branches of big trees, perhaps in a place where the bark had curled, or in a knothole.

"It was magic, like when a performer makes a bird appear from out of his hat," he told me. "These birds could smell the smoke from miles away."

Or when they made those long fishing expeditions, having stopped for lunch on the shore of some salmon pool—the guests fished while he cooked—the jays would appear from out of nowhere.

Through the late fall and early winter, one of those jays gathered so much confidence in my father that it ate bread and doughnuts out of his hands, and in doing so, bonded a spiritual chemistry with him. My father grew to love the bird.

One day, when the jay was eating from my father's palm, thinking he could domesticate it, he grabbed it by the feet—in the way that one might playfully grab and hold a lover. The bird flapped its wings and its little two-fold whistle turned into a mournful screech. Daddy said that he could feel its heart pulsing as he looked into its eyes, so dark and wild and beautiful.

"They were like marble buttons on a wool sweater," he told me. He stroked the white and grey feathers on the bird's throat and back, in the way he might have cuddled a kitten. And then he set it free.

Dejected, the bird flew into a tall tree. My father watched as it righted its ruffled feathers. And I could imagine its stilted plumage as it roosted in the bare, grey limbs of November, its long, straight tail feathers like broom strokes in new snow. This took a long time, and when its task was completed, the bird flew away. To my father's great sorrow, he never saw that beautiful bird or any other Canada jay at the lunch site again. He set crumbs in the woods around the fire's smoking ashes, thinking that maybe the jay would come around after he left the woods for the night. It never came. Obviously, it had been an assault on the bird's soul—more damaging than a wound to the flesh—betraying even its family's trust in him.

My father told me that moose-birds, four to six inches tall, nest in the late winter in snowy, foodless conditions. Their eggs incubate in temperatures of minus thirty degrees. Its fluffed-up feathers keep the nest warm. They mate young and stay together as long as both the male and female live. They eat many things including berries, insects, and in winter, rosehips and spruce seeds that fall upon the snow.

I can remember the inquisitive Canada jay coming from out of the trees in April to take my crumbs—like a Eucharist—when I ate my bread and jam sandwiches in the yard of our little one-room school at Keenan. The schoolhouse was so near the woods that our teacher warned us against wandering off and getting lost if we left the playground. At lunchtime, if she did not see all fifteen of us in the yard, she came out on the steps to give the bell an angry shake. As a small boy, I fed a part of my lunch to the jays each day, even in winter, especially in winter. Back in the classroom, Mrs. Underwood lectured us on the importance of being kind to all birds and animals, that the Canada jay especially was a soul bird, connected to the spirits of old relations long dead, as well as a sacred symbol for the First Nations peoples. This was an important part of the day's lesson. Even when we hunted squirrels in the woods, we refused to throw a stone at a moose-bird. We were so near to the land and to nature back then that the jay was a part of our curriculum, this bird and the poetry of E. Pauline Johnson, W. Wilfred Campbell, and the stories of Harwood Steele and Grey Owl. Upon reflection, that old school with its Canadian poetry, its storied playground, and eating out of doors with soulmates, is looked back upon as the very best of times.

I remember Mrs. Underwood saying that the Canada jay was a member of the crow family—hard to believe—and one of the most intelligent birds of the air, indeed, a defining part of our wilderness. She claimed the bird was trustworthy and had a mournful mating song, though seldom heard as they travelled in pairs—male and female—through life. They lived to almost twenty years old and were found in all provinces and territories.

To me the Canada jay is a spirit as much as a creature, a friendly Canadian voice, kind, melancholy, even sentimental in its plight. Like a true Canadian, this bird is humble and will take a backseat to birds that are more ostentatious, vocal, majestic: the bright-coloured blue jay, the eagle, the snowy owl, or the robin.

I had been thinking about these things when I heard the news that the Royal Canadian Geographic Society has chosen the Canada jay to be our national bird. I am thankful that I have the spirit and soul of this bird in common with my fellow countrymen. Shall we see it on a coin perhaps? On a paper note? That would be fine with me. But I hope I never see it on a hockey jersey. Like a piece of scripture in red ink, our national bird is too sacred for commercialization.

Now, as an old man, for a sense of comfort and healing, to escape the rat race and capture a bit of soul nourishment, even in winter, especially in winter, I go beyond the frozen river, beyond those huckleberry school grounds, beyond the inspirational words of old school readers, beyond the now invisible fences of December farms, to my own inherent woodlot. There beside Morse Brook, where black water flows among black alders, I build a fire on the ground, have a good cup of tea, feed and talk to those old-world, omnivorous jays whose forebears would have communicated with my own lineage. I have given them names: David, Tom, John. Yes, that spirit bird of my boyhood is still here.

"Bad luck to kill a moose-bird," Papa always said.

ACKNOWLEDGEMENTS

The Introduction, "More Than a Sport," is used by permission from Jake MacDonald as it is taken from his anthology, *Casting Quiet Waters: Reflections of Life and Fishing* (Vancouver: Greystone Books, 2014). The essay "My Miramichi" appeared in the summer issue of the *Atlantic Salmon Journal* in June 2016. "Fishing the High Country" appeared in the fall 2016 issue of the *Atlantic Salmon Journal.* "Afterword: The Moose-Bird" was published as "In Praise of the Canada Day" in the *Telegraph Journal* in December of 2016. "Fishing the Gray" appeared in the winter 2017 edition of the *Atlantic Salmon Journal.* "The Deep and Dark Dungarvon" appeared in the spring 2017 edition of the *Atlantic Salmon Journal.*

I would like to thank my first readers, Heather Browne and David Adams Richards. I am also grateful to Pete Blair, Dennis Duffy, Tim Trabon, and the staff at Trabon Group of Kansas City for their design of leaflets and the poster contributions.

I would like to acknowledge the sources of the following material: On p. 18 excerpt from Leonard Shengold, "A Third Literary Example — Sergei Aksakov," in *Haunted by Parents* (New Haven, CT: Yale University Press, 2007), 166. On p. 78 excerpt from Marcel Proust, *The Modern Library In Search of Lost Time*, vols. 1–6, translated by Terence Kilmartin, C.K. Scott Moncrieff, and Andreas Mayor (New York: Random House Publishing Group, 2012). On p. 200 , Anton Chekhov, "About Love," in *About Love and Other Stories*, translated by Rosamond Bartlett (Oxford: Oxford UP, 2008).

Wayne Curtis is one of New Brunswick's finest nature writers. Born and raised along the Miramichi River, his writing evocatively brings the river and its landscape to life.

Curtis is the author of seventeen books, including three novels, five collections of stories, and six books of essays, among them *Fishing the Miramichi*, *River Guides of the Miramichi*, *Wild Apples*, *Of River and Earthly Things*, and *In the Country*. His writing has also been published in numerous magazines, literary journals, and newspapers, including *Quill & Quire*, *Fly Fisherman*, *Outdoor Canada*, *Eastern Woods and Waters*, *Maritime Sportsman*, the *National Post*, the *Globe and Mail*, and the *Telegraph-Journal*. His stories have been dramatized for CBC Radio and Television.

Curtis's work has been recognized with a number of awards, including the David Adams Richards Prize and the Atlantic Salmon Federation Conservation Award. He received an honorary doctorate from St. Thomas University in Fredericton in 2005, the Order of New Brunswick in 2014, and the Senate of Canada Sesquicentennial Medal in 2018.

He divides his time between his apartment in Fredericton and his cabin on the Miramichi.